# It's *All* About Love

## A Life Explored

Margaret McElrath

ISBN: 0-9990902-0-8
ISBN-13: 978-0-9990902-0-6

# DEDICATION

This book is dedicated to my earthly siblings.
May you find Peace and Contentment in the most unusual places.

# CONTENTS

# ACKNOWLEDGMENTS

I am very grateful for the myriad forms of support I have experienced along my journey and want to thank everyone who has befriended me, listened to me, strengthened me, loved me, offered thoughts of encouragement and provided practical editorial, grammatical and punctuation corrections for this book. (The critics have been helpful too!)  Primary to my sustenance is my steadfast husband whose love, devotion, architectural and cooking skills are extraordinary. We are blessed with two amazing daughters – Heather and Erin – whose hearts are as big as all out doors with minds equally beautiful and open. I have grown closer to my brothers Ken and Robert as the years have advanced and our lives tacked through different storms. Rosie and Robin and Cathy and Trish and Bill and Margaret and Tony and Lorraine and Shirl and Clare and Dian and Kathy and Tina and Alford and Lucy and Ina and Gail and Susan and Deb and Michelle and countless others have contributed to my well-being, my growth, my book, and my contentment as a human being. Thank you from the bottom of my heart!

# PREFACE

At 43 my world turned inside out, upside down and backward. No, I didn't experience an automobile accident that left me a quadriplegic. This fallen-away Methodist got the answer to a prayer.

I considered myself the most normal sort of California progressive woman with a college degree, loving husband, two healthy children and a challenging career. But I was miserable in my own skin.

I was a middle manager in the Information Technology (IT) industry supervising the development of custom software. The systems got bigger and more complex as software languages matured and computer hardware and memory became cheaper, more efficient and powerful. Unfortunately, it's very difficult for those in the IT trenches to keep pace with a management perception that tools, megahertz and massive amounts of storage can make the creative process faster and easier.

One of my favorite IT cartoons has two ants reviewing a complex flow chart of a software system. The supervisor is pointing to a specific process that seems to bring the entire picture into focus. However, upon closer examination, the process proclaims: AND THEN A MIRACLE OCCURS. The supervisor's pointer directs our attention to that process box and he proclaims: "I think we need a little more detail here."

That cartoon served as a metaphor for my life at that stage: a complex flow of events and cross roads meandering through the years, with event-by-event connection, but little understanding of where it all was headed. Channeling this process was my subliminal hope – and then a miracle occurs – and I live happily ever after.

Like the cartoon ant, I had come to a juncture in my life when my "supervisor" knew that I needed a few more details. And as philosophy promises, when the student is ready, the teacher will appear.

This student was ready for another perspective and no amount of reflection on what I already had, deterred me from taking a hard look at my angst. I knew that there had to be something more. I knew that I had more to offer, more joy to experience, and more living to explore. I just didn't know where to begin. Driving home from work one evening, I made a heartfelt request to the universe: "God, help me understand what this anxiety is all about." It didn't take long for my prayer to be answered in a series of events and revelations that I could not have imagined or orchestrated in my wildest dreams.

The next several months would completely scramble my personal story and clarify the impact forgotten and buried lifetime events still have on me today.

My story may not be too dissimilar from yours. We may have more in common than either of us can imagine. I hope so. Not that I consider my life such an ideal model. But as human beings, the emotions and events which make us human – make us family.

Like my daughters, who are so similar and so different at the same time, I believe that we humans are more similar than we are dissimilar, regardless of our geography, politics, economic strata, or sexual orientation. We may be opposite sides of the same coin, but we are the same coin: male, female, gay, transgender; young, old; Protestant, Catholic, Jew, Muslim, atheist; democrat, republican, libertarian; blue-collar, white-collar; aristocrat, working-class. We want joy and happiness for our families and ourselves; we want a comfortable living space; we want food on the table; we want healthy, happy children; we want peace. We experience joy, sorrow, pain, anger, envy, and love. We love.

But love is not always the sugar plum, cuddly babies, and romance sort of love that we most readily associate with that emotion. When consciousness needs to be raised and intervention imperative, tough love is as loving in the final analysis as the romantic comedy sort that Hollywood banks on. And so that you will not be lulled by the title of my book thinking this another motherhood-and-apple-pie sort of story, I will tempt you with a spoiler: my story unfolds along the tough-love path.

Our daily world draws attention to our dissimilarities. I hope my story draws attention to our similarities, our common humanness. I write to share some insights I have discovered along my journey. My insights may seem obvious to you; they may also seem right out of left field. They have taken time and serious reflection to appreciate. Each layer of my understanding further defines my perception of love, and gives me yet another layer to explore and comprehend – the proverbial onion.

It has taken me over 25 years to digest the events, make sense of them, and put them into a context that sustains me. I am well aware that what I want to share may distance some of those who today I call friends: in fact, that is the paramount reason it has taken me so long to publicly commit my experiences and reflections to writing. For those of you who choose to hear me out, I hope it will inform and provide insights you may not otherwise have considered or been exposed to. And by association, provide clarity for aspects of your life and others' lives that will allow more charity and compassion to prevail in dealing with all manner of humanity.

The soul in me believes that when we finally master the love lab work that spiritual leaders throughout civilization have taught to often distracted students, then truly, a miracle *will* occur, and we will *all* live happily ever after.

Margaret McElrath

# FREE WILL

I'm Monday's child: August 23, 1948, 6:50 a.m., Pomona Valley Community Hospital, Pomona, California. And at my current stage of life, I recognize that grace has been a constant companion.

I grew up in the San Bernardino Valley in Southern California. We moved to a house on East End Avenue in Chino when I was 3 or 4 years old. I do not have many memories before that except for the memory of an elegant staircase that I was not allowed to climb on the property where we lived. Early in my parent's marriage, we occupied a renovated hen house on a farm owned by friends of my maternal grandmother. This was early, post World War II and housing was at a premium.

The house on East End Avenue was a very stable part of my childhood. Unlike my eldest daughter who moved 15 times in her first 18 years of life, I had my first dolly cake in that house; I hosted teenage parties in the family room; I said good-bye to many well wishers when I journeyed to Sweden for my junior year of college; I had my wedding reception there after the cake and punch at the church; and I gathered with relatives and friends on East End Avenue after my father's funeral.

Our home was on two-thirds of an acre, with wonderful dirt for growing vegetables and children. We dug forts in the back yard and hunkered down to hide from our friends playing hide and seek. Dad built us a huge swing set from galvanized pipe and elbow joints that he bought at the local hardware store. That A-frame was the center ring for several back yard circuses that I organized and staged. We performed daring feats on the swing, paraded our pets in silly costumes, and sold popcorn and lemonade for a nickel. We persuaded the corner convenience store to sell us some small, brown candy bags to use as containers for the popcorn we prepared in the kitchen. Our popper was the heavy aluminum bottom of a pressure cooker we pushed and pulled across the gas element to create the white kernels.

The corner store was a great source of penny candy and nickel gum packs. On summer afternoons we bought popsicles, jaw breakers, 5-cent Milky Way and Snickers bars, and Tootsie Rolls – my all-time favorite. My brother got into trouble once for cashing in a coke bottle that did not belong to him for the return-pennies. I honestly do not remember how mom and dad found out, but I may have blocked the memory that I was the snitch: I was a miss-goody-two-shoes at the time and Ken and I were scrapping siblings. The corner store always had whatever run-up-and-get-me-some mother needed to finish a recipe she was in the middle of for dinner.

Our back yard would never have been called manicured. There was a clothes line that had four separate lines for hanging wet garments, and more length than we ever had clothes to fill. My father built a small hot house behind the garage to grow orchids that was partially underground: the roof was glass and above ground. He replaced it with a cement patio slab after one of the neighborhood children fell through the roof, climbing up to take a look inside. Mike was not seriously hurt – a few cuts and bruises – but the incident and fear of more serious injuries gave my father the motivation to take the hot house down so there wouldn't be a next time. Years before the hot house disappeared, Dad would turn anonymous plants and orchids into corsages for Mother's Day or some other special occasion, for Mother, Grandmother or a family friend. It would not be until he retired that my father returned to his passion for growing orchids.

We also had fruit trees, a strawberry patch, and a conventional garden when the strawberry patch became too much work. Mother grew roses and camellias. There was a walnut tree on the back-forty that provided crunch for hundreds of batches of cookies. Dad grew boysenberries and grapes. Mother canned apricots and peaches from fruit trees on the back-forty. We would have the most wonderful peach and boysenberry cobblers in the summertime. Years later, a Black Turkey fig tree was planted near the Rio Oso Gem peach tree. Dried, candied figs became a favorite Christmas treat.

I have very early memories of my father killing chickens by wringing their necks and of the stench of chicken feathers submerged in boiling water to make them easier to pluck – I got to help. There were rabbits grown for eating and petrified rabbit skins hung on the walls in the garage years after we got all of our meat from the grocery store. I never quite managed to gain an appreciation for the clams Dad would bring home after fishing trips to Pismo Beach.

Mother always cooked. Even when she worked full time, we had three-course meals and dessert nearly every night of the week. She never ordered pizza or Chinese take-out. We always had table cloths and ate on china, even at the frequent Girl Scout and Boy Scout potlucks. Sunday dinner was especially bountiful and served on the good china. I grew up seeing food grown, preserved, and presented on pressed linen and in porcelain vessels.

I was a very curious child and often drove my parents to distraction: I always wanted to know "Why?" of every conceivable subject matter. And as overworked and impatient as parents often are (myself included!) it's instructive to note that my father's favorite response to one of my why-questions, was "Cat fur to make kitchen britches." And more often than not, that declaration effectively shut me up. It was delivered with conviction which did not invite further inquiry. So I was often left to my own wits at discovering the things I was curious about. I have always been more an observer, than participant – an introvert in the Myers-Briggs scheme – so although he could shut me up, he couldn't turn off my mind.

My very earliest memory of thinking "Why?" must have been at 3 or 4 years of age.

Mother took me into the only bathroom in the house where my father was showering and sat me on the toilet. I didn't think it out of the ordinary until my father shut off the water, and pulled the shower curtain aside and said, "Don't you think she's getting too old to be in here with us?" And at that admonition, I noticed my father's penis for the first time, and it surprised me. I said nothing, but still remember the mental gymnastics I went through. *I don't have one of those: what's it for? It can't be to go potty – I don't need one: it's more like an arm or leg.* I finished my private analysis with a matter-of-fact conclusion: *it has to reach somewhere.* But I never spoke these questions or thoughts. Sex – or nudity for that matter – was not a subject that was ever brought up or discussed, which probably isn't especially unusual given the 1950s time frame.

The day I discovered that there was not a real Santa Clause, brought more "Whys?" to the fore. The occasion was a phone call from my grandmother asking me to spend the night with her; one of my favorite things to do. In my zeal to get ready, and without first asking permission, I raced into my parent's bedroom to get the black and white checkered suitcase that I always used for such occasions. As I popped open the suitcase, I found doll clothes and dresses with lace and puffy sleeves, partially sewn. I intuitively knew what I had just exposed. I hurriedly closed the suitcase and carefully returned it to its hiding place and nonchalantly asked my mother, a safe time later, which suitcase I should use. I never let anyone know what I had discovered, and I don't remember whether the black and white checkered suitcase was carefully emptied and given to me to take to grandma's; that was an insignificant detail. I had been totally shaken by my discovery.

I waited to see where those dresses would show up, and sure enough, there they were, Christmas morning, on my dolls. And sure enough, Santa Clause got all the credit. I still remember wondering previous Christmases why Santa always brought me the nice presents, and why I only got underwear and pajamas from Mom and Dad. I thought it strange, even as a child, that someone I did not even know, bought me nicer presents than my own parents. This year the fraud was uncovered in the most innocent of events, but with a keenly remembered sense of sadness. The sadness wasn't that I had lost a Santa Clause. The sadness was an incredulous, "Why did they lie to me? Why did they let Santa Clause get the credit for the doll clothes? Why didn't they want me to know that they liked me more than underwear and pajamas?" I wondered these things in silence, knowing that no one would be interested in how I really felt. I already knew I was expected to be happy for what I had, and I dutifully obliged.

I also remember the humiliation of having to sit with the principal, Miss Williams, when we went to get our polio shots. I always fainted – went crashing to the floor – and would have to be revived with smelling salts and sit in the front of the bus where Miss Williams could ensure that I was all right. Of course I always was, and I always knew I would be fine, but grownups do not believe you at 6 or 7 when you tell them that. *Why don't they believe me?!* So I never got to sit with my friends, and my propensity for fainting became legendary with the teachers. The pattern repeated itself every time shots were administered. As an adult I understand the concern: but as a child, I felt unnecessarily singled out and treated differently, and I did not like the feeling.

(Needles have bothered me all my life. I have a childhood memory of ascending a flight of stairs and hearing a blood-curdling scream from another child behind the door at the top of the stairs. Mother had taken my brother and me to the county's well-baby clinic to get immunization shots. The Clinic was at the top of a flight of stairs in one of the county buildings in Pomona. It was not until the fall of 1994 that I discovered how a memory got attached to the immunization needle: a story I will share later.)

One other childhood medical event retains a significant "Why?" component.

The standard in the 50's was to take out children's tonsils at the age of 5 or 6. I do not remember the doctors or nurses or any specific pain: I only remember the lie. They told me that I would get to eat as much ice cream as I wanted, after getting my tonsils out, as a reward for being a good girl and cooperating. What I distinctly remember is feeling so lousy that I did not even **want** ice cream. I remember feeling deceived.

It was not the last time I wondered why somebody had not told me the truth. Why didn't they think I could handle it? The **truth**, that is.

One final, childhood memory is noteworthy and actually quite vivid. It happened on a visit from Uncle Duke and further strengthened my growing analytical muscles.

Uncle Duke was my father's much-younger, half-brother. And although nothing specific was ever said, my mother's disdain for Uncle Duke was obvious. She was always polite, always ready with a meal or coffee and cookies, or whatever the situation called for, but there was reluctance in her civility that was palpable. The best part of my uncle was his wife, Aunt Alice, who Mother obviously cared for. But in years to come, Alice would divorce Uncle Duke, remarry, and my cousins' step father would legally adopt Duke's three children, forever removing his surname from their lives. There must have been a few heartbreaking stories behind my mother's scorn.

The day I remember, was actually quite serene and affable. I was probably 8 or 9 years old. While Mother finished the lunch preparations, the living room buzzed with family chatter and the usual what've-you-been-up-to questions and recent narratives. I recall other adults in the room, but my memory does not serve to identify them. Uncle Duke was returning from a show in Las Vegas, where he had a lounge act that sounded special and important and seemed to overshadow the lives of the other adults in the room. I had a vague idea about Las Vegas (this was southern California) but little appreciation for lounge acts or anything else that Las Vegas offers.

Uncle Duke's good looks, charisma and gift for engaging conversation, enhanced his talent as a hypnotist. He was quite proud of his act, the celebrities he rubbed elbows with, and eventually offered to give the family audience a demonstration. Would anyone care to be hypnotized?

I was swift to volunteer. Not that I can tell you my motivation. I was usually pretty open to new experiences and this sounded like an interesting proposition. Besides, at that age, I was certainly into the art of pleasing adults.

Everyone settled down and Uncle Duke sat me in a chair in the corner of the room, making sure I was comfortable. He then proceeded with a pendulum movement, to dangle a round-shaped item that looked like a necklace in front of my eyes. I don't remember exactly what he said, but at some juncture he declared I was "under" and proceeded to go on with his mini-show.

He announced that he was going to bend my arm. He *could not* do it. His strength as a grown man did not budge the elbow of an 8-year-old. He made other announcements and proceeded to display his control over my every move.

He declared that he would hold a flame under my arm and it would not burn me. He clicked a cigarette lighter and held the flame about a half-inch away from the tender skin of my forearm. I did not flinch nor was there a blister or any trace of a burn.

My mother freaked out! Leaning on the edge of the pocket door into the kitchen, she shrieked her displeasure. She insisted that Uncle Duke stop immediately and waited for him to oblige. When he did not, she retreated into the kitchen where she remained until the show was over.

And this is the fascinating memory: I was in complete charge of my "state." I *knew* that I had the option to come out of the hypnotic trance, or stay exactly where I was and continue with this adventure. I was also keenly aware of my mother's distress, but completely aware too, that it was **my** decision to come out of the trance, or stay put. As much as the adult Uncle Duke was driving this demonstration, I knew I was not doing anything that I was not fully aware of and agreeing to on some level. Uncle Duke had not taken over my mind: he had just tapped into a level of my 8-year-old consciousness over which I had no previous knowledge or understanding. But I was safe and not threatened in any way.

So I chose to stay hypnotized, and also, quite unlike me, defy my mother's call for control. This was certainly a case of exercising my God-given right of freewill. Had I chosen to respond to her fear and not my own curiosity, I might never have followed that curiosity 35 years later, when I had a real desire – and need – to understand something that was more serious than the antics of a Las Vegas lounge act.

I am not sure where it comes from, but I have an insatiable need to understand "Why?"

# DEATH

A surrogate grandmother – Grandma Hendricks – presented me with my first experience of death. The Hendricks family belonged to my father's lifelong best friend Nick, who he had met in junior high school, and would share army duty in Pearl Harbor on December 7th as well as be at his bedside when he died in 1986. Having moved to Chino when his parents sent him away to live with an uncle, the Hendricks were the closest thing my father had to a caring, extended family throughout his adult life.

Grandma and Grandpa Hendricks actually lived down the street from us on East End Avenue and had a chicken ranch. I don't remember many extended family gatherings there, but I remember stopping regularly with my father to pick up eggs and visit for 15 or 20 minutes. Grandma Hendricks always had a bear hug and cookies and was happy to see us. Grandpa Hendricks, originally from Holland, prided himself on his tulip beds, which were unprecedented in southern California – the winter weather was never cold enough to help the tulips deliver their best in the spring. Grandpa's secret garden tool was an old refrigerator in the breezeway. After the tulips had bloomed and their greens withered – ensuring enough stored energy for the next growing cycle – grandpa would dig up the bulbs and store them in the refrigerator until late fall, when he would plant them again for the spring showing.

I remember being relatively unfazed by Grandma Hendricks's death. It was quite usual if being old and sick and having lived a good life, logically preceded the final solemnity of a church service, and a graveside burial. I was probably ten or eleven at the time, and while I cried and shared in the family's loss, the events followed the human story as it's told over and over again so it didn't evoke any soul searching or stimulate any questions: it was merely a testament to this-is-how-life-works.

That was not the case when my 22-year-old cousin Bruce died fourteen years later when I was a young wife and mother.

Unlike the vague memories of family events with the Hendricks, holidays, birthdays, and other special occasions were spent with aunts, uncles, and cousins on my mother's side of the family. Gertrude Martin, the matriarch, had moved west from Chanute, Kansas, with her husband and two toddlers in a Pullman car that delivered them into the Pomona Valley sometime in the late 1920's, early 30's. The transplanted Kansas farmers established a new home base, which ultimately gave way to suburban sprawl and office buildings. After her marriage to my father, Mother settled in Chino not 5 miles away. Uncle Earl moved to Redlands, about 30 miles away, and Uncle Walt went 2-plus hours north to Bakersfield. Rarely did we celebrate in Bakersfield, which always annoyed Uncle Walt, since "…the road goes both ways…" he would often chide.

Uncle Earl and Aunt Jane had an orange grove in Redlands that provided plenty of space for outside play with cousins who were only a few years apart in age. The tractor gave the young boys driving lessons that probably improved their skills on public roads when they were old enough to get their licenses. I will always remember the grafted tree in the front yard that produced both oranges and grapefruit. Cousin Chris gave me a haircut in the den that horrified my mother and Aunt Jane. We enjoyed frequent family gatherings and didn't have many cares to speak of. No one would have called us well off, but such things didn't faze us at the time and so we just played, created memories, and ate lots of good food.

Things changed quite significantly when Cousin Bruce was diagnosed with muscular dystrophy, around the age of eight. I remember Bruce without his wheelchair, but those memories are old and few and during his remaining 14 years, I would never again see him without his chair. But if anyone could make the best of the situation, certainly it was Bruce.

The orange grove gave way to a new freeway in southern California, and the coincidence of the diagnosis and real estate windfall meant that Bruce would have the best care possible and not destroy the lifestyle of his parents and older brothers. Uncle Earl, a gymnast and health devotee, was physically capable of attending to Bruce's living requirements. It was common to witness Uncle Earl lifting Bruce for bathroom breaks, but Bruce's evolving health issues never interfered with family gatherings and from all outward appearances, Bruce lived a very normal life. I'm sure my aunt and uncle sacrificed a great deal caring for him, but if they complained or felt burdened, I never witnessed any grievances. They installed an in-ground swimming pool in the backyard to help with physical therapy. Bruce attended the neighborhood schools, had lots of friends and participated in school and church choirs. After high school, he enrolled in college and attended regularly. One of my favorite stories involves three of his high school friends kidnapping Bruce in a van one weekend to give him a surprise trip to Las Vegas. Initially alarmed, Aunt Jane and Uncle Earl were soon reassured that his friends would take very good care of him, could handle his physical needs, and would make sure he took his meds. Bruce returned unscathed by the adventure and grateful for the love and devotion of his friends: his family was impressed too.

In November of 1974 however, the disease took its ultimate toll, and Bruce died in the comfort of his home, surrounded by family and friends. The death certificate indicated death from pneumonia, which seemed unfair to let muscular dystrophy off the hook. But the reality is that the disease destroys the lung muscles making breathing extraordinarily difficult and the immune system incapable of fighting the process. So pneumonia was the ultimate grim reaper.

I had a two-year-old at the time and life was full and expanding. Bruce's death was a significant struggle for me, irrespective of my Methodist upbringing and recognition that death was an inescapable aspect of life. I was not happy with God!

"Why Bruce?"

"Why such a young person?"

"What did he do to deserve such a short life?"

"Why did Bruce have to get muscular dystrophy in the first place?"

"Life is **so** unfair!"

My father was more philosophical.

"Did Bruce live a good life?"

"Yes."

"Was Bruce loved?"

"Absolutely!"

"Didn't Bruce love and care about others?"

"Of course, and he had lots and lots of friends to prove it."

"Would you say that Bruce had a full life, even though it may have been cut short, from your perspective?"

"Yes. There was hardly anything that his friends and brothers did that he didn't do too."

"Can you imagine that there are people in their 80's or 90's who haven't lived as full a life as Bruce has lived in 22 years?"

"Probably. A long life doesn't mean a quality one."

"Then maybe there's another answer; another way to understand what may be happening."

"OK. And what would that be?"

"Have you ever heard of reincarnation?"

"No, not really. What would reincarnation have to do with Bruce and muscular dystrophy?"

"Well, what if Bruce had been responsible for causing someone to lose their ability to walk in a previous life? 'Karma' as it's called, would mean that in another lifetime, Bruce would need to choose to have the experience of not being able to walk to understand fully what his previous actions had actually done to that other person."

"I'm not sure I follow."

"I'm certainly not an expert on the subject, but many people believe that over many lifetimes, our souls return to earth to experience the consequences of our human interactions, both positive and negative. Someone might get away with murder – at least they might not be apprehended and sentenced in a court of law – but reincarnation and karma would mean that the soul would have to experience 'murder' in another lifetime to fully understand what effect they had had on another's life. They would personally experience what they had *created* by their actions. I don't know how all the details work, but that's it in a nutshell."

To say I was intrigued would be an understatement. I remember thinking: If someone did something that harmed someone else, whether there was a law against it or not, they would never get away with it. *I liked it!* It certainly made more sense to me than a seemingly arbitrary lottery of perks and damnations that defined my existing set of beliefs about what life was all about. What seemed to matter more than anything was the sense of *fairness*. Ultimately, no one would ever get away with "murder," or any other crime against humanity. And generosity and kindness would reap rewards.

I would soon have lengthy conversations with my father and we would create our own mini book club and enjoy philosophical discussions that I had never before entertained. I found **Yoga, Youth, and Reincarnation** by Jess Stern, and began a serious inquiry into a newly found awareness.

Margaret McElrath

# AWARENESS

Bruce's death and the awareness of another way to think about life spurred my interest in reading as much as I could on the subject. My husband did not share my curiosity for metaphysical titles, but remarked in solidarity, that he was glad to see me reading.

I spent the next 17-plus years immersed in the genre, as much as you can immerse yourself while working full time. I still managed a household that grew to include 5 horses, a goat, and a cat. Work-related assignments moved us across the country three times in 12 months. And when we finally settled permanently on the east coast, we brought another daughter into the world.

Jess Stern's book had introduced me to Edgar Cayce and for several years, I was a member of the Association for Research and Enlightenment (ARE) which keeps Cayce's 14,000 psychic readings available and relevant for metaphysical students around the world.

There were books by Deepak Chopra, Raymond Moody, Shirley McLain, Jon Kabat-Zinn, Wayne Dyer, Elisabeth Kubler-Ross, Jane Roberts, Louise Hay, Dan Millman and many others. One book was highly recommended and gifted by my father: *A Course in Miracles*. (I would discover years later, contrary to my assumption, that he had not given either of my brothers a similar keepsake. The book eventually brought me personally close to a colleague who had come across the text via his own journey.)

Software development management on a contracting basis is a frustrating business relative to employee continuity and building corporate knowledge. It is not uncommon to lay off one set of software engineers with office automation skills and turn around and hire another set with mainframe, large-systems skills to meet the specifications of the next contract. Retraining software engineers often is not an option. From the onset, projects need journeyman-level expertise in a specific engineering discipline and toolset, not rookie trainees. One of the more difficult patterns of my work involves laying off engineers with one skill set and hiring another team with different skills.

My job is always on the line too. Will the profit margin be adequate? Will the new business come along at a pace commensurate with the expectations of the marketing department? Will we have the tools and technology budget to optimize what each engineer can produce? Will someone get his feelings hurt and threaten to kill his colleague with a hunting knife? Will I have to fire one of the engineers I just hired because his interviewing skills were superior to his technical ones? These are the things that stress software engineering managers with the job of creating custom software. And those are just the professional ones.

On a personal level, it's keeping up with day care for my five-year-old and school activities for my high school senior. It's laundry, housekeeping, dinner and all manner of minutiae that my propensity for taking care of the details demands. I am scheduled from morning to night in an attempt to stay one step ahead of my to-do list. And it's not getting any easier; the burn-out is beginning to show. There's an extra 50 pounds on my 5'6" frame, no time for exercise or planning a healthier lifestyle. It's just getting through the day that consumes me.

I am reading more metaphysical and self-help books in an attempt to bring some calm to the chaos. I have again picked up the copy of **A Course in Miracles** my father gave me, and I am trying to understand its expressions of forgiveness and other, seemingly inverted but enlightening concepts. I have three or four different books on my night stand that are in various stages of completion. My search for a more serene life looks as unlikely on the night stand as it does in the light of day.

My career is something I treasure for all its frustrations. The company I joined in the late 80's received an unsolicited buy-out offer from Cincinnati Bell Information Systems. My role in the corporate takeover was insignificant, but memorable. As a middle manager, I enjoyed several evenings of excellent dining and entertainment intended to introduce the managers from both companies to each other. The CBIS CEO struck me as a thoughtful and experienced business man who was genuinely excited about the synergy he anticipated from the corporate marriage. His synergy platform was expressed in every speech he gave and permeated corporate communications during the takeover.

Cincinnati Bell was an independent telephone company even before the divestiture of AT&T. At the time they purchased my employer, they had a 120-year business history that began as Cincinnati Telephone and Telegraph. The buyout made a handful of people independently wealthy, but as a mid-level project manager, my few shares of company stock might have given me a few weeks of R&R, but my greatest benefit was an opportunity to learn a new industry, and to meld into a larger corporate culture, and discover telephony skills and nomenclature. I was never disappointed with the deal.

Soon after my employer was bought, the contract for my project was lost to a lower bidder. I grabbed onto the synergy platform of our new corporate leader, and with my vice president's support, flew to Cincinnati to meet with project managers on the NTT project and test the synergy philosophy in a very tangible way. I returned to Fairfax with a new project and requirements to hire a software engineering staff to support the efforts in Cincinnati.

\* \* \* \* \* \* \* \* \* \*

"Hello."

"Oh! Hi. Welcome. It doesn't seem like it's been a week and a half, but it must be. Here you are."

I grabbed a manila folder from the corner of my desk that contained Jeff's new-hire paperwork.

"Come with me. I'll show you the office space where you'll be working. Here. You'll need to fill out this paperwork to get the system IDs you'll need to function. Deborah can show you the ropes."

"Deborah, Jeff. Jeff, Deborah."

"You'll be sharing this office for the project. Deborah can also give you tips on the local sandwich shops and show you where the office supplies are kept. The company orientation isn't scheduled until 2:00 PM this afternoon. Let me know if there's anything you need. I have a quick staff meeting every Monday at 10:00 AM in my office. See you in a bit."

\* \* \* \* \* \* \* \* \* \*

NTT – Nippon Telephone and Telegraph – Japan's telephone company, contracted with CBIS in the early 1990's to build mainframe-based COBOL software to run an entirely new telephone system in Japan. The NTT Project encompassed the development of a full suite of software systems to support the operation of ten regional telephone sites in Japan, and consolidate service that was highly decentralized and managed by hundreds of small, community telephone companies. CBIS had significant experience with every aspect of telephone operations; everything from plant management and cabling to network management and customer service and the development of software to support each of those components. That experience and a long-standing business relationship with NTT, secured CBIS a one-billion dollar software engineering contract to replace the telephony infrastructure in Japan.

My mission was to build a team of software engineers to assist the Cincinnati engineers from Fairfax, Virginia, build components of the Customer Service software suite. The demands of the project, which expanded at one point to over 750 people, had drained the Cincinnati area of available software engineers. Moreover, at that time, mainframe software development was done alongside business operations, which always impacted the pace and coding cycles software developers could expect. With the addition of a T1 line (business-speak for an industrial-strength phone line) between Cincinnati and Fairfax, my team was be able to write software using a local area network, upload the software for nightly compilations with modules from our project colleagues, and receive error logs and changes to file definitions and business rules the following morning. Cincinnati got a fresh set of engineers and was able to off-load software development tasks they were otherwise unable to accomplish. Fairfax got a new project and revenue stream, and I remained employed. It was a win-win scenario for all concerned. The NTT Project turned out to be a pivotal time in my career and ultimately my life.

* * * * * * * * * *

"You OK?"

"Yes. Sorry! Does it show?"

"Doesn't look very 'OK' from where I stand"

"Well, I'm having a bad day. But I'll be OK. Always am."

"Can I help?"

"No, Jeff. Thanks for the offer. I'll be fine."

"OK. Is this a good time to talk about a couple of things?"

"Sure. What's up?"

"I tend not to be a morning person and would like the flexibility to come in around 9 and stay later in the evening."

"That shouldn't be a problem. I need software, so as long as the work gets done, I have no issue with you coming in at 9. I understand that the creative juices don't necessarily flow on demand between 8 and 5. Is that all?"

"No, I'd also like to set up a process for staging our software so we can get a better handle on integrating our modules with Cincinnati. I think we'd be better off if we do some additional testing before we upload our code. We're getting errors that we could avoid if we just staged things a little differently. I can explain it to the others during the next staff meeting if you're willing to take a chance with my suggestion."

"I'll be happy to support whatever efficiencies you – or anyone else for that matter – can offer to improve what we're doing. You know we have a unique development environment. We don't have to share the mainframe with production work and compete for processing cycles. Cincinnati doesn't have the flexibility we have, but anytime we do something new it's bound to have its problems too. Just let me know if there are any issues."

The business expertise Jeff had relative to telephony was exceptionally helpful since I had never managed a software project involving telephone systems. Jeff had worked with AT&T for years and his knowledge about writing software to handle telephone accounts and deal with the myriad permutations of calling plans and the ultimate creation of a monthly phone bill were invaluable. We would have to deal with billing addresses in Japan that were completely foreign to our American expectations. There were party lines in rural areas that defied a standard methodology for delivering bills and accepting payment. City apartment complexes had entirely different addressing structures. Due to the extensive number of local offices in Japan, phone company staffs personally knew their constituency, regardless of living arrangements. A software system built to function in regional centers however, had to somehow codify neighborhood culture into bits and bytes that translated into repeatable, predictable results. It was not a trivial business or software engineering challenge.

Jeff became a key member of my staff and our professional relationship included morning coffee confabs and grabbing lunch together on occasion to discuss design and project issues. And as fastidious as I try to be to keep my personal and professional lives separated, my escalating personal angst could not be totally hidden at the office.

I eventually discovered that Jeff had a propensity for intuiting personal issues and providing counsel: he had an uncanny ability to listen. He had had a particularly difficult childhood and was sensitive to other people's issues. His personality was not intent upon fixing something, but he listened, and was capable of intelligent insights and attuned to thinking out loud.

On one occasion I mentioned my struggle with *A Course in Miracles* and discovered that Jeff was very familiar with the curriculum, and had been a student of the *Course* and other unique metaphysical ideas for years. That mutual study became a door that opened a more personal relationship: a relationship that would evolve over the next several months into friends and confidents. Jeff and I were kindred spirits.

During one of our lunch-hour conversations, I tried to understand a concept that was everywhere in my night-stand books, but one I did not fully comprehend.

"What's my 'higher self?'"

"What do you think it is?"

"That's why I'm asking!" – frustrated as I often was at Jeff's Socratic approach to every conversation.

"I don't really know. Sometimes it seems like the author is talking about my conscience. Other times it sounds like some sort of alter ego or cosmic connection to another dimension. It's similar to my confusion about enlightenment. Is enlightenment a goal, something you actively strive for like a new job: or is it something you ultimately acquire like gray hair? The lexicon of terms doesn't make the concepts any easier to understand. I think I understand and then I read something else, and I'm back to square one. What do you understand 'higher self' to mean?"

"I think ultimately, like so many things, you have to *experience* it to *know* it. But for me to explain my understanding, context is important."

"I believe that we were all born with a specific purpose, and that purpose is a God-given direction for our life. Can you accept that you were born with a purpose?"

"Yes. It's just not clear that I've ever discovered what it is."

"No matter. The important thing is that you accept the premise of having a life's purpose."

"Yes. I buy that."

"Another concept that contributes to context is that as human beings, it is in our best interest to have a sort of amnesia about the spirit world so we can function on the earth-plane."

"I'm still on the fence about that. But for the sake of this discussion, I'll suspend my skepticism and accept that that is the case."

"God doesn't send you into the world without a safety net. It would not be a loving thing to do, and if God is anything, he is Love. He accompanies you on your journey through life using a connection to the universal plan that simply said is your higher self. It's sort of an invisible partner, fully cognizant of your spiritual purpose, which keeps you connected at an unconscious level to your divine map. Your higher self is a tangible, personal connection to God."

"So it's not my conscience or a part of my mind?"

"Not really. It's not part of you, but it's connected to you. Sort of like the internet, which is not you, but you're attached to it. It's a reality that touches everyone, but not everyone is connected, if you understand what I mean. God gave us free will, so your connection to your higher self is only at your invitation: the internet exists, but you have to choose to be connected. And unlike your conscience which has been conditioned to feel guilt and other man-made shame, God's love and guidance is available to you at all times, but you have to ask for it. You have to trust and invite your higher self to introduce herself to you."

"So how do I recognize when it's my higher self and not just me – thinking?"

"Your higher self – your *aware* self – does not sound like you – thinking. It has its own 'voice' that seems to come out of nowhere at times, but it doesn't provide you a weather report or neighborhood gossip or parental nagging. It will never abandon you and you will recognize her by the nature of her message. You will learn, with attention and purpose, that your higher self is not you – thinking.""

"I noticed that you clarified 'higher self' by calling it my 'aware self.'"

"Higher connotes something above you. I want you to think of it as an intimate part of you; as normal and essential as your gallbladder or pancreas. Your aware self is not hiding; not something you seek and find, but something you *discover* that was there all the time. You have no conscious knowledge of your pancreas, but it's there and performs its function whether you are conscious of it functioning or not. Recognizing your aware self just takes acknowledgement and a trained ear to distinguish her from the other things in your consciousness that are far from Godly."

"I think I prefer aware self: it suits my sensibilities. I'll try to be more open to an encounter. Is there anything I can do to encourage her to show up?"

"No, she's always with you. Your aware self is not likely to chat and carry on lengthy conversations. She is typically brief and to the point. She's probably been 'talking' to you for years, when you have soulfully asked for help. You may just not have recognized her voice or influence. She can be helpful beyond your imagination. But you will have to be open and non-judgmental about whatever she has to say. You may not always like the message. But as the saying goes, 'Don't shoot the Messenger.' Your aware self is a spiritual gift and deserves your respect."

\* \* \* \* \* \* \* \* \*

"It's time."

Click went the remote and the credits for **Rumpold of the Bailey** were gone.

I reached over and turned off the lamp on the bedside end table and laid down my book. Off came my bed wrap and I eased down under the covers and into my husband's warm embrace.

"I love you."

"I love you too."

Our legs intertwined under the comforter and we moved closer, burrowing into each other. I felt John's gentle strength and reveled in the security of the moment. I lifted my head from his chest to get a kiss, and knew John was interested in more than a goodnight peck.

"You have such soft kisses" he purred, and the delicious moment evolved into the love making we thoroughly enjoyed. Patient, gentle petting escalated the moment.

"Come. You get on top" interrupted our foreplay, and the familiar dance continued.

As we played with each other and inched closer and closer to a climax, I failed to notice the public address system being turned on in my head.

**YOU ARE GOING TO RUN NTT.**

Not only did I not climax, I reacted with a jolt that only an unwelcome Charlie horse would warrant.

"Are you OK?"

"Yea. Yea, I'm fine" I insisted and grabbed the memory of a Charlie horse to transition the moment. I immediately rolled onto my side of the bed and stretched my leg as memory served.

"I'm so sorry! I got a Charlie horse in my butt and it ruined the moment."

In fact, the public-address-system message had shocked me to the core and I was not only speechless, I was dumbfounded and couldn't calm down. My heart was racing as though I'd just escaped a head-on collision. Metaphorically, I guess I had just had a head-on collision with my aware self.

I turned over to John with a reassuring hug and lay there, totally wired, my mind racing a mile a minute, and unable to sleep. We would not resume our play, but John was understanding and turned over to sleep without protest. It wasn't long before I recognized his gentle snore and knew he was sound asleep.

It would be hours before I settled down.

I gingerly crawled out of bed so I wouldn't wake John. He didn't stir. I left the bedroom, closed the door behind me and curled up in the easy chair on the landing and wrapped myself in an afghan.

I'm going to run NTT?! No way! No how! I can't do that job! I don't have the experience! I wouldn't know where to start. I was incredulous at the concept but no less incredulous at the communiqué.

Who was the messenger?

*I* couldn't be the source! I've got a healthy ego, but this wasn't the result of wishful thinking – I didn't know what it was about, but I could not mistake the message: **YOU ARE GOING TO RUN NTT.** Six little words out of nowhere kept me awake until 3 AM when I finally accepted that I had not been hallucinating. I had inventoried all my faculties and found them intact. However, I was incapable of knowing what it all meant.

I guess you could say that at a minimum, making love with my husband at least removed the rationalization that I had made up this voice in my head. It certainly aligned with Jeff's admonition that my aware self doesn't sound like me – thinking.

Margaret McElrath

# EPIPHANY

The NTT project was becoming more and more intense. Deadlines loomed while critical requirements were still being negotiated. Many of our requirements were delivered third- and fourth-hand from our Cincinnati colleagues who worked directly with the customer business analysts from Japan. I finally negotiated a seat at the requirements table so we could ask questions and get input directly from the customer. Requirement meetings in Maitland, Florida became routine.

A corporate meeting delayed one of my Maitland trips and put me on a later flight than my colleagues. Moreover, since corporate resources book travel in date and time order, I ended up staying at a different hotel, which meant I would not be running into my team at breakfast or dinner. But that wasn't all bad. My free time would likely be mine – a welcome perk.

"Come. Let's go get lunch. You need to buy a book," Jeff said in my office doorway.

"Ok. Give me a minute to wrap this up."

Jeff and I and hurried through our salads so we could spend some time in the book store.

"Here it is. *The Drama of the Gifted Child*. You need to read this."

Jeff had recommended several books in the time we had been

having lunch and serious conversations. So I grabbed the copy from his hand, added it to the two books I had already picked up on my own, and went to the cashier to check out. My Florida trip was planned for a week, so some reading material unrelated to work was welcome.

*The Drama* is a relatively thin book. It went into my carry-on so I could get a head start the plane. I was not prepared for its impact.

Jeff had not given me any indication about the nature of the book. I surmised from the title that it had something to do with intelligence, as in the high school Gifted and Talented Program that accelerates the curriculum for the students who can handle more advanced material. (*The Drama* actually had a similar effect, come to think of it.)

But my concept of "gifted" was not validated by the text. Rather, it touched a very deep, emotional core in me that I had never acknowledged or recognized before.

Author Alice Miller's premise is that there are children gifted with an ability to intuit their parent's needs, at the expense of their own, and proceed to give the parent what he/she needs, for an incalculable price. It's an inverted relationship.

I had never in my life read any book that spoke to me with such emotional clarity. Welling up with tears, I read deeper and deeper into Miller's treatise. She was talking about me as if she had been an invisible friend on my shoulder for many, many years.

I didn't finish the book before we landed. I had to pause and reflect too often to rush through the text, but the freedom-from-colleagues evenings allowed me to finish the book during the week and examine a layer of my constitution I had never considered.

The week passed quickly with long, intense sessions that were punctuated with language struggles: our male Japanese counterparts worked through an interpreter (female) that I found interesting on several levels. For while the interpreter was very adept at both English and the lexicon of software and telephony jargon, it was also obvious that the Japanese analysts understood a great deal of English.

The signs were subtle, but there were knowing nods at critical junctures even before the translation, which seemed to defy the need for a translator. Maybe this was some sort of psychological game that was supposed to give the NTT analysts an upper hand. Regardless, I was grateful that my team was a part of this requirements gathering session and fascinated with the foreign laptops that generated kanji character sets and graphic diagrams at the touch of a key. (This was the early 90's.)

The week passed quickly and the work progressed faster than we had expected, so I called the airport and was able to book a late Friday morning flight back to DC. As I entered the cabin, the first over-head compartment on the left was open to reveal a stash of magazines – our steward invited everyone to take one or two for the flight. Since I had finished the two books I had brought with me, I grabbed one of the three visible copies of *Lears* and found my window seat near the rear of the plane. I was pleased that no one sat next to me and the flight was unusually light, a detail for which I would later be extremely grateful.

"May we have your attention" signaled that we would soon be off the ground and home-bound.

I took a deep breath, reflected briefly on the events of the week – both professional and personal – and closed my eyes for a nap.

"Mam. Something to drink?" The words startled me out of my restful grogginess. Sleep would not return.

I sat my ginger ale on the drop-down tray in the middle seat so I could cross my legs in comfort from my window perch. I reached for the *Lears* magazine I had grabbed when I entered the plane and casually leafed through the pages. I read a personal biography and then turned to the article that changed my life.

The article was about incest, a subject I had never read anything about. I understood the concept, but it seemed bold of *Lears* to include such an article in a popular magazine. I finished the article and focused on the side-bar that contained signs that were common among victims of incest. The sidebar suggested that if several of the indicators were true, incest might be a life experience of the reader. It further suggested allowing a thoughtful period of six months or so to consider the possibility and then to seek professional counseling if something emerged. Adapted from a checklist by E. Sue Blume, the following fit me to a tee.

1. Gastrointestinal problems, GYN disorders
2. Wearing a lot of clothing, even in summer: baggy clothes; failure to remove clothing even when appropriate to do so; extreme requirement for privacy when using the bathroom
3. Need to be invisible, perfect, or perfectly bad
4. Anger issues: inability to recognize, own or express anger; fear of actual or imagined rage
5. Rigid control of thought process; extreme solemnity or humorlessness
6. Boundary issues: control, power, territoriality issues; fear of losing control; obsessive/compulsive behaviors; attempts to control things that don't matter
7. Guilt, shame, low self-esteem, feeling worthless, high appreciation of small favors by others
8. Feeling demand to "produce and be loved" – instinctively knowing and doing what the other person needs or wants
9. Compulsive honesty or compulsive dishonesty (lying)
10. Alienation from body—not at home in own body: failure to heed signals of body or take care of it; poor body image; manipulating body size to avoid sexual attention

I read each item slowly and deliberately. I was both fascinated at the concept that such an experience could be distilled into a checklist and simultaneously appalled at the truisms that defined me. My feedback would not take six months to adjudicate.

Within seconds, my body memory erupted in the most disturbing rage I had ever experienced, and over which I had no authority. My tears flowed uncontrollably. I desperately searched my purse for Kleenex to sop up the flood. I was shaking and trembling hysterically. I tried to control my reactions, but the more I tried the more out-of-control I felt.

"Who could have done this to me" I asked as I searched my memory banks for clues to this consuming rage. A family friend recently had passed away and I wondered if the reason I was not drawn to attend his funeral was prophetic. Could he be the one?

**THAT's TOO EASY!** Trumpeted the knowing voice of my aware self.

I was not willing to consider another alternative, but I felt compelled to answer. The **Lears** article had exposed the likely suspects.

"My father?!"

There was no audible response from my aware shelf — none was needed. My body told me the truth — the rage escalated into writhing vibrations that echoed in every cell of every limb. I was experiencing a rage that I had never known myself capable of. It was devastating and irrepressible.

At the height of this burning rage, my aware self interjected: **REMEMBER. HE ALSO GAVE YOU** *the COURSE*.

Surprisingly with that declaration, the rage melted almost as quickly as it had emerged. There was a catharsis and cleansing that I had never experienced, nor even imagined. The most poignant result of this epiphany was my ultimate healing.

*There's nothing wrong with me!* My conscious mind acutely realized.

And that was more profound than anything my 43 years of living had discovered. What made that revelation so meaningful was that it was not even something I was consciously seeking. But the insight healed years of subtle, inner loathing.

Subconsciously I had carried a silent burden, simply stated: I am flawed. In the course of a split second, it was clear that there was truly, nothing wrong with me. I had lived my life attempting at every turn, to create proof of my worthiness, to anticipate criticism with accomplishment, and mask my imagined flaws with piety. It was now perfectly clear that those attempts had been entirely unwarranted.

A kind stewardess noticed my distress, offered me some much appreciated fresh Kleenex, and asked if she could help. I motioned her away, barely able to speak, but confident I would be OK. There was precious little time to pull myself together: the plane had already begun its descent. John would be picking me up at the metro after I landed at National Airport and I didn't quite know how I was going to answer his predictable question: "How was your trip?"

# INQUISITION

It was a beautiful, late-spring afternoon when John met me at the Vienna metro. I was somewhat surprised but delighted to see that he had driven the Austin Healey, top-down, to pick me up. The drive home would give me some extra time to think, since the road noise in the convertible made it impossible to carry on a conversation.

"Are you OK? You look like you've been crying."

"Yes. I'm fine. I'll tell you about it later."

But the twenty minute commute home did not inspire any further insight into my rather eventful flight. I'm not one for sugar-coating things or beating around the bush, and my emotional state, to say the least, was rattled to the core. So when we arrived home and took my suitcase into the house, I shared the crib notes of the last few hours.

"I just had an indescribable epiphany on my flight home that my father sexually abused me as a child."

"Impossible! No way! Your dad could never do that. You must be imagining things."

I knew I had not imagined the last few hours, and the sharp rebuke from John was not unexpected. A part of me had had the exact reaction and intellectual disbelief. But the healing that accompanied the revelation was unmistakable: the healing – that was as real as it gets!

I dropped the subject and busied myself with unpacking and

getting up to speed on the domestic activities I had missed while I was in Florida. I didn't press the issue or seek to convince John. I was still very conflicted about the insight I had just unwittingly received and I needed time with my own thoughts to figure out where this new information would take me.

This was August 1991 and my father had passed away five years earlier—March 1986. We had been very close, especially in my teenage and young-adult years, and before I married I would have called him my best friend. From an early age, he told me I could do absolutely anything I put my mind to, and he was always supportive of my extracurricular activities and school work. My father was not a man I could imagine sexually abusing me. I wondered more than once if through some sort of neurosis I had made this all up, but that made no sense either.

My father always seemed a much happier person than my mother, which didn't make much sense until I was in high school and discovered that when my brother and I were very small, probably 3 and 4, Mother was told by Dad's doctors that he had less than 3-months to live. He had been feeling poorly for months, but no one could figure out what was wrong. Finally, he was diagnosed with lung cancer (Army-induced, two-pack-a-day smoker) and the prognosis was very bleak. As luck would have it however, there were clinical trials for experimental cobalt radiation treatments for lung cancer at Pomona Valley Community Hospital, and Dad was admitted to the trials. Unbeknownst at the time, he was cured and lived another 35 years before passing away from another form of cancer. He shared with me at one point that although he was never able to purchase life insurance, as soon as he received the diagnosis and a *name* for his ailment, he intuitively knew he was going to be just fine. Optimism was a hallmark of his character: I cannot remember a time when he was angry, depressed, or even particularly sad.

Dad was not quite 6 feet tall – probably 5'10" – 5'11" in his Sunday shoes. He was never over weight, which was the condition for everyone in the family except me. And while Dad was never overweight and probably on the low end of what was considered a healthy weight for his frame, he never did any serious physical exercise to add strength, adjust his diet to minimize calories, or adopt any exercise routine to enhance his physique.

Dad was a redhead; Welsh heritage we are told. There are pictures of him as a young man with mounds of hair. In his later years he was bald except for the band of hair from ear to ear under his hat brim that is typical when age is the barber. He never had a beard or mustache. His red hair and fair skin translated into whiskers that were meager and light-colored, so even if he had grown a mustache no one would likely have noticed. His skin was highly sensitive to sun and when we went to the beach in the summer, he would always wear long pants and long-sleeved shirts to shield him from the burning rays. I remember one particular camping trip to San Clemente when Dad did some fishing from the sea shore. He was fully covered from head to foot, except for his bare feet wading into the retreating surf to cast his line. As luck would have it, the tops of his feet got so burned they blistered and wearing shoes proved painful for weeks.

Dad's countenance was unremarkable. He had a comfortable but erect stance. He never stooped even with age. He wore glasses and a non-descript wrist watch. His wedding ring was a simple, unadorned band. He was never one to dress to any fashion standard or statement. He never wore jeans or wing-tip shoes for that matter. He had a cloth hat – not ball cap – with a stitched 2 inch brim that he was seldom without. But his Sunday best never included a topper. He had one suit and several ties that filled all of his social requirements. I remember him primarily in khaki-colored pants, patterned, short-sleeved shirts, a belt, and a cloth, waist-length jacket. I never remember him having a long coat or rain slicker. There was a plastic poncho that came with us on vacation trips in the Sierra Mountains, but one basic wardrobe suited all four seasons in Southern California.

Our home on East End Avenue sat on two-thirds of an acre, so we grew fruit trees, a vegetable garden, grapes, strawberries and boysenberries and Mother's roses and camellias. My father had not come to the country life naturally, although he took to it quite readily. Dad was handy around the house building an additional bedroom, bath and family room on East End Avenue shortly after my younger brother was born. Brother Ken and I were in Scouts, but younger brother Robert joined 4-H and tended sheep and their offspring in the backyard. Dad supported each of us and our many extracurricular projects. He was a modest and quite conventional sort of man.

Dad's own father had banished him to an uncle's care in the country for reasons I will never know. What I know of my grandfather wouldn't take thirty-seconds to reveal. Dad shared once that he was told as a child that he wasn't "wanted." His father had actually wanted another daughter. Mother also disclosed when Dad was nowhere in sight, that my grandfather had been killed in a bar-room brawl.

My father was an usher in church and occasionally volunteered with the Methodist Men. His Army service in Hawaii introduced him to orchids, a passion that ebbed and flowed over the years, culminating in a florist supply business when he retired. Retirement also saw him taking in various stray cats, befriending and feeding them; only occasionally allowing them to come inside. He always said he hated cats.

What purpose would it serve to vilify a man I truly loved, that my husband and daughter, mother and brothers loved? What purpose could I have for maligning a person whose funeral was well attended by relatives and friends and adorned with gorgeous flowers from his business clients? Nowhere in my experience – schooling, or relationships with neighborhood friends and relatives – was the word incest ever uttered.

I racked my brain for clues that might help me sift through these contradictions. A few things eventually came to mind.

I remember a statement Dad made that I totally rejected, but found curious regardless. He said, "Children do not have memories." I don't remember the context, and I know that I don't have volumes of childhood memories, but I could not accept that as true.

Also there is a dream-like memory staring at him at waist-level adjusting the strings in his pajamas. It's a partial memory: that's all I see, and I am not looking at his face, although I know it's my father. My memory is that I'm staring at his waist as he's actively cinching up the drawstrings of his pajamas.

As a young child, I was constantly taking Milk of Magnesia. My father would usually administer the tablespoon of white, liquid chalk for my upset stomach; usually during the night. It became such an issue when I was in third grade that my mother made an appointment for a complete upper and lower GI study. I don't remember that the procedure was painful; just boring and time consuming. I remember having to take a thick pink liquid (that reminds me today of Pepto-Bismol) and sit in an inclined chair while it wound its way through my system. What is still odd for me to remember is what Mother recounted after the results were tabulated. "The doctor said he found no evidence of a disease, but commented that your study looked more like what he would expect of a 40-year old woman, not an 8-year old child."

My father was an amateur potter, and considered himself somewhat of an artist. He actually taught pottery for evening, extended-education classes. When I was somewhere between 8 and 10 and we were alone in the house (I don't know where my mother and brothers were, but we were definitely alone), Dad went to a corner cabinet in the family room where the laundry basket was kept, and retrieved an over-sized, hard-back, glossy, coffee table book – probably an inch thick – and proceeded to sit next to me and leaf through the pages. He stopped when he came to several nude photos that were taken with breasts and nipples poised skyward. He seemed to be trying to convince me of the *art* the mountainous landscape represented. He was trying to educate me about nude photos being art – which as an adult I have no issue with – but as a young girl, I still remember rolling my eyes and thinking to myself, "Yea, right!" And that's the end of my memory. I don't remember putting the book away; just my rather disgusted reaction, "… just who are you trying to convince?!"

As a young mother, while changing my daughter's diapers one evening, Dad instructed me to massage my infant's genitals: "It's good for her. She'll like it." Later that night, I remember asking the universe's forgiveness for not following my father's instructions to fondle my child. "I know God that I will make all sorts of mistakes as a parent. You'll just have to add that one to the list if it's in fact something I should do. I can't do it. I can't imagine how it can improve her well-being."

One adult memory, however, is the most disconcerting.

Early in our marriage, we moved to Davis, California, so that John could attend graduate school. We ultimately bought a house, sold it after a few years, and made plans to build a custom home on a lot east of town. We lived in an apartment complex after we sold our home while we waited for the new house to be built. My parents came up one weekend to see the building progress, and as was routine for us, Dad and I went for a walk and a conversation. These conversations usually consisted of a review of a new book or metaphysical discussions that were of no interest to either my mother or John, so a private walk kept everyone happy. And just as I can remember where I was at the time of JFK's assassination, I can remember the spot in the parking lot of our apartment complex where Dad said to me: "I wish your mother had been a better lover."

I know I protested that I didn't want to hear such things and we certainly did not engage in a lengthy conversation about my parents' love life. I knew it then, but had never been honest with myself until now: my father's proclamation was not a casual, off-the-cuff statement of fact. It was a thinly veiled apology for using me for his own sexual needs. I was 28 years old at the time and I had buried the memory of that declaration in a shallow grave, unable at the time to hear my father's real message. The events of the last few days reminded me of the conversation 15 years previous and "apology" was the unmistakable message he was delivering at the time.

I was very grateful for the diversion of weekend chores and yard work to keep this incessant, internal investigation at bay.

My epiphany was always in the background however, and I did not engage John in my examinations. He had made it clear that it was not a discussion he wanted to have. I was initially hurt and felt let down by his attitude. I thought it was "… for-better-or-worse." And this certainly was the worst I'd ever experienced. Isn't your spouse always supposed to be there for you? But after some very serious reflection, I recognized that John wasn't trying to be cruel or ignore my distress. He had had a wonderful relationship with my father, and compared to his own father's workaholic-induced absence in his life, he considered me very lucky in the father-lottery. So asking him to work through this with me would be a very conflicting thing for him to do. And I had to grudgingly recognize that the universe had already given me all the sounding-board help I needed. My kindred spirit Jeff was not a fluke supplement to my life: he was a deliberate cosmic gift in this emerging drama.

I was very curious to know what Jeff would make of my epiphany. He obviously did not know my father, but I knew he would have some perspective.

I grabbed Jeff for lunch on Monday and shared the events of last Friday's flight back to DC and the ensuing remembrances that had surfaced. I had at least expected some sort of shock or surprise reaction, but he listened to my story with an inert demeanor as if I were reciting a grocery list or something just as innocuous.

"I remember you telling me during one of our early conversations that you had had a happy childhood. Well, just for the record, I have *never* connected with anyone who had a happy childhood. I knew then you were in for a big surprise down the road. I guess that's what happened on Friday. Surprise!"

Jeff could be annoying! His humor was not always appreciated. But he listened and could *hear* what I had to say and not think me hysterical or vindictive. I am very grateful that the universe put me in his way.

Margaret McElrath

# CONTEMPLATION

I would compare the next several months to a twilight zone of sorts. I had no clarity or plan and confusion and skepticism reigned supreme.

I vacillated between wanting to know more details about my buried childhood and being truly grateful that I was relatively unscathed by the epiphany as confirmed by my present situation. I was in good health with no serious dysfunctional habits: alcoholism, drug addiction, cutting, or other self-destructive behaviors – things I learned are common among incest survivors. I was doing work I thoroughly enjoyed, earning a comfortable salary, and living in a loving and satisfying family situation. The healing had been real and could never be reversed, so leaving this episode behind, was one rational approach.

But there were so many unanswered questions.

Why had I blanked out the incest? What mechanism was that? Am I somehow making this entire story up? And if I am making this up, what's my motivation? Why now?

If this did happen, where was my mother? Did she know? Did it happen to my brothers? Where? How?

And the most compelling question of them all: if this is karma – my current experience created by my actions in a previous lifetime – what the hell did I do to warrant incest?

Jeff remained a valuable sounding board and we had numerous subsequent conversations. Deborah, Jeff's office-mate, was also becoming a friend as she inquired about *A Course In Miracles* and other metaphysical books. We became a mini book club, sharing the latest read and discussing the implications at the water cooler.

Deborah and I met up for breakfast conversations on weekends and occasionally shared lunch dates during the week. I revealed my epiphany with her and we bonded over her very tangible memory of physical and verbal abuse as a child.

Early one Sunday afternoon, there was a knock on the door and there stood Deborah with a book in her hand.

"I'm supposed to give this to you."

"What?!"

"I bought this book yesterday, and a voice in my head said 'Give this book to Margaret.'"

"Come in. Why don't you start from the beginning?"

Deborah came in and we went into the family room for a conversation.

"My brother's birthday dinner was last night, and I was ready more than an hour early, so I decided to go to the book store and look around to kill some time before heading over. When I picked up this book, a voice in my head said 'Give this book to Margaret.' I was miffed and thought no way: it's my book. At which the voice repeated itself in no uncertain terms: GIVE THIS BOOK TO MARGARET. So here I am with the book that *you're* apparently supposed to have. But I want it back when you finish so I can read it too."

"Of course! I don't expect you to buy books for me. But you have to admit the guidance is a bit unusual!"

But the timing was impeccable. The following day I was headed again to Florida for several more days of requirements gathering. I was happy to have another book to read, and the curious delivery made the book that much more intriguing.

The book was *Many Lives, Many Masters*, by Dr. Brian L.

Weiss. I carried it with me on the plane and within 48 hours had it devoured. Dr. Weiss is a traditionally trained psychiatric physician, who graduated from Columbia and Yale Medical School. In his practice, he had a chance encounter with a patient suffering from panic attacks and multiple anxieties that changed the direction of his career and her life. He unwittingly uncovered the potential of hypnosis therapy to heal the present effects of past lives by asking his patient under hypnosis to tell him where the problem began: it had begun in another century.

One of the other reading materials I had tucked into my overnight bag, coincidentally, was a copy of the monthly magazine from the Association of Research and Enlightenment, ARE. The following month a weekend seminar was scheduled featuring Dr. Brian Weiss, Dr. Raymond Moody, and Dr. Robert Jarmon. I marveled at the synchronicity of it all, and vowed to show the advertisement to Deborah when I returned to see if she would join me. Not too surprisingly, it didn't take much to convince her. We called-in our registration and booked a room in Virginia Beach.

I had no knowledge of Dr. Jarmon, but I had read a number of books by Raymond Moody and was excited to know that he would be sharing the billing. My father and I had read and discussed a couple of his books, and one of Dad's promises to me, based on our metaphysical pact, was to somehow communicate from the afterlife, a subject Dr. Moody had been researching and investigating for years. I had no clue how that was supposed to happen, but Dr. Moody believed that such communications are possible and it would be interesting to hear what he had to say as well as hear from Dr. Weiss directly. Unfortunately we discovered that the session Raymond Moody would be hosting was already booked, so we would not be able to participate in that particular seminar. That information from the registrar was disappointing to say the least, but not enough to derail our enthusiasm for the weekend.

We arrived in Virginia Beach late Friday evening after a long, stop-and-go drive from northern Virginia. I had returned the book to

Deborah and we had both consumed its message. We enjoyed discussing the implications en route.

The Saturday Morning session was hosted by a member of the ARE staff, welcoming everyone, lecturing on reincarnation and Edgar Cayce's take on the subject, and setting the mood for the weekend. The seminar crowd numbered several hundred, consuming every chair in the meeting hall. ARE staff and other standing-room-only participants added to the sum total of attendees. The crowd was primarily in the over-50 age bracket, but there were a handful of people in their 30s and 40s. The schedule was announced, room assignments acknowledged, and meals would be on our own. Dr. Moody would be speaking after the lunch hour, and Dr. Weiss later that evening with Dr. Jarmon.

Deborah and I made a hasty retreat after the morning session since we wanted to get to the ARE bookstore and peruse the titles: we were devouring books at a healthy clip and constantly looking for another title to add to our collection and expanding awareness. We were delighted by our incredible good fortune to look up from the tables and hear a member of the ARE staff welcome Dr. Raymond Moody.

Dr. Moody was kind enough to share some time with the staff that was otherwise not able to hear his lecture in the afternoon. For the next 40 – 45 minutes, we heard the essence of Dr. Moody's lecture and his theories about how we might be able to communicate with deceased loved ones. The serendipity of our timing to visit the library having been excluded from the seminar's lecture due to our late registration galvanized my sense that Dad had somehow arranged this synchronicity and Dr. Moody's ideas would ultimately lead to my ability to communicate with him in another dimension.

Dr. Jarmon opened the evening session, discussing various aspects of hypnosis and the positive results of regression therapy. What stands out in my memory was not his lecture per se, but his recitation of Max Earlman's 1927 poem, *The Desiderata of Love.* I remember quite spontaneously bursting into tears when he read one of the lines: "… you have a right to be here." I decided to ask Dr. Jarmon for his business card at the break, and noted this portion of The Desiderata on the back. It would take an internet search when I got home to capture the entire poem for future reference.

*Many fears are born of fatigue and loneliness. Beyond a wholesome discipline, be gentle with yourself. You are a child of the universe no less than the trees and the stars; you have a right to be here. And whether or not it is clear to you, no doubt the universe is unfolding as it should.*

Dr. Weiss's lecture did not disappoint. His peaceful, gentle demeanor is still memorable, as was his genuine desire to help people. I was quite impressed that he was not in a hurry to leave the lecture hall, and an hour and a half after he had concluded his remarks, Dr. Weiss was still autographing books and chatting with everyone who cared to approach him.

Before the lecture concluded, however, Dr. Weiss performed group hypnosis. I had no problem going into an altered state of consciousness in the course of his hypnotic monologue. My state took me to a scene in what I intuited as the Middle East. This is what I remember from the regression.

I am an older man, maybe in my 60s, who is relatively healthy and clean. I am not a pauper but my surroundings are modest. I have a small, dirt-floor, white-washed home with windows open to the air – no glass or cloth cover the opening – and I am wearing all white clothing and have sandals on my feet. My stature is relatively short and I am not skinny, but neither am I rotund. I have a little extra weight on my frame, so for my age, I am healthy and well. I have no sense that I live with anyone, but my "job" is to protect and watch out for the young boys playing in the square. The hypnotic state doesn't let me know why I am there to watch out for the boys, but in this state of consciousness, it's clear that my role is protecting these boys. It's a very strong, unambiguous communication under hypnosis.

Dr. Weiss then instructs us to go to the end of this lifetime and view our death.

I am not much older, but I die on the dirt floor in a corner of my home, what feels like a natural death: no violence, no illness per se, just a passing in my sleep.

I didn't have any sense that this lifetime had anything to do with my current situation, but it was an experience I found totally engaging and I was definitely leaning toward having more regressive hypnotic experiences to see what that state could tell me about my current situation and other past lives.

In less than three years I would have the opportunity to again attend a seminar in Virginia Beach and experience a past life regression with Dr. Hazel Denning and put this puzzle-piece into a larger context. I was just beginning my journey back to the future.

# BODY MEMORY

The seminar in Virginia Beach was the tipping point. If I had any reservations about looking into my past, the lectures and group hypnosis confirmed the value of pursuing the unknown.

And if you are wondering whatever happened to my aware self's forecast that I would run the NTT project, it didn't happen. But that's an interesting sidebar that ultimately had value too.

Jeff and I talked about business matters often with as much intensity as we did the spiritual ones. On the subject of me being able to run the NTT project, his Socratic prodding, edged me away from my not-me cliff with some very pointed and soul-searching dialogue. I realized over the course of several weeks, that I just might have the experience and temperament to handle the job, albeit the job would certainly be a stretch and challenge beyond anything I had ever encountered. And that was his point.

"Where's the challenge if you continue to do projects that are safe and repetitious of projects you've already accomplished? Surely you're not afraid of growing through a new challenge?!"

Ultimately I came to realize that I would not turn down an offer if I got a call from Cincinnati. But the call never came, and the project wound down rather abruptly. However, before I was notified about the project shut-down, I had a curious dream event as I was awakening one morning before work. I tried to go back to sleep and recapture the moment, but it was to no avail. A kindly, well dressed older gentleman appeared out of nowhere and announced in no uncertain terms: "Your assignment has changed." It would be many weeks before the project came to its abrupt conclusion, but when it did, I was not really surprised.

So the responsibilities of a large-scale software engineering project did not materialize and my familiar routine returned: find new project, lay off staff with no transferable engineering skills, and hire new staff for the new project. Jeff fell into the lay-off category and although we stayed in touch for awhile, he had completed the engineering and spiritual job I believe the universe had sent him to accomplish. I have not heard from him in years.

The Virginia Beach conference marked the beginning of a focused research mission about my immediate and past lives. I wanted to both validate that the incest had not been a figment of my imagination, and I needed to know what past life connection my current situation reflected. I would have liked to work with Dr. Weiss, but trips to Florida from the DC area were not practical. I was favorably impressed with Dr. Jarmon and since he lived in New Jersey, that trip would mean a much more reasonable distance for me to travel on an occasional basis. I phoned Dr. Jarmon and made an appointment.

Dr. Jarmon had said it would take about four hours from the DC area to Spring Lake. My appointment was set for 1:00 pm. I left my daughter at day care at 8:35 and arrived only a couple of minutes late after two wrong turns not a mile from his office. My appointment was scheduled for two hours.

I had never in my life had an appointment with a "shrink" and it was not an easy thing for me to do. I pride myself on my ability to solve problems and this incest/reincarnation thing was just another problem to solve, so I surmised. I recognized too, that this was not only new territory for me: it was also an area of inquiry that was not in mainstream medicine, or popular culture. I really didn't have the faintest idea how I would go about finding a hypnotist willing to regress me in the DC area, so my choice to see Dr. Jarmon was not a difficult one to make. At least I knew he was open to the research. My colleague Deborah was still willing to talk with me about metaphysical ideas and share and discuss books on the subject, but she was the only one at the time willing to do so. Getting some expert help/advice from someone who had already crossed the medical threshold into metaphysics seemed a prudent and reasonable thing to do.

The session was like any first-visit for a physician: parent-sibling family history; spouse-children family history; personal medical history; pain levels; anxieties; medications; etc. It's a 45-minute to an hour exercise that stayed true-to-form with Dr. Jarmon.

Once these preliminaries were out of the way, we got down to the reason for my visit, and what I hoped to accomplish.

I shared my epiphany and experiences since I had said my prayer on the way home from work one evening, and expressed my desire to first make sure I wasn't somehow making up the incest. I also expressed my desire to delve into possible past lives to understand where my current circumstances had originated. I recounted the ARE seminar where we had first met.

Achieving a hypnotic state is not particularly difficult, when the subject is willing, which I certainly was. (I suppose it can be laborious if there is fear and pushback.) Dr. Jarmon began with a relaxing monologue and then a deliberate coaching segment, inviting me to go deeper and deeper into the relaxed state. Once hypnotized, Dr. Jarmon directed my attention through a series of routine questions about time, place, and surroundings. As the session progressed, and as I discovered the pattern over time, his questions became dependent on what I was experiencing and relating. Sessions typically concluded with positive affirmations and counsel to support me, as the hypnotic state withdrew.

This first time, I was half fighting the hypnosis, half letting go. At one point, I remember saying to Dr. Jarmon that I didn't think I was under. But before he brought me back I had relived the very real memory under hypnosis I had confided to Dr. Jarmon when he took my medical history, was my worst fear.

I am probably 5 or 6 years old. It's night time. I am sleeping. I awaken when my father enters my bedroom. I try to turn away, pretending to sleep. But he obviously is not fooled and is stronger and bigger than me. Turning me onto my back, he proceeds to kneel over my body. I am soon pinned to my bed under his weight, immobilized in fact – and in fear – while he thrusts his penis into my mouth. Under hypnosis I gasped for breath. The inside of my mouth became very moist with an unpleasant taste. I felt the inside of my mouth stretch to accommodate his penis. I was totally and utterly helpless. (I was pinned to the chair in Dr. Jarmon's office as motionless as I had been in my bed, so many, many years earlier.)

And this was not the first time: it felt all too routine. The memory ended finally as I watched my father standing up in the dim light of the cracked bedroom door, cinching up the drawstrings of his pajamas and leaving. There was no conversation, no words of comfort, only intense, helpless feelings of betrayal; and very real, profuse sobbing.

I have read that the human body has its own memory bank, and this episode made me a true believer. I was feeling everything I had experienced in my bedroom well over 35 years before, more than 3000 miles away in California, as if it were happening in that moment in New Jersey, in the over-stuffed leather chair in Dr. Jarmon's office

Dr. Jarmon supplied generous amounts of Kleenex and explained that the healing process included facing each of these old ghosts, not knowing how many there would be, realizing that each time, there would be one less standing in my way. He said I was doing well: that some of his patients had taken years to get to this juncture in their healing process.

I made another appointment for the following month and was evasive about wanting to face each incident of abuse in subsequent sessions. I knew I still needed to know more, and would continue to see Dr. Jarmon until that need was satisfied.

Dr. Jarmon commented at the end of our session, that when he was in medical school (my guess would be late 50's, early 60's), incest was believed to be an event that occurred maybe one time in a million. Today, he revealed, the statistics support the statement that one in four women have experienced incest. (*The Courage to Heal* states that one in three women and one in seven men are incest survivors.) Dr. Jarmon also stated that without exception, *all* of his patients have experienced some form of child abuse.

I think we have a major problem here.

Margaret McElrath

# DIRTY DRESS

With some foreboding, I traveled to Spring Lake for my second session with Dr. Jarmon about a month later. I trusted Dr. Jarmon and felt comfortable in his care under hypnosis. But I had experienced my worst fear on my first visit: what was I heading for on my second?

I had spent some time contemplating Dr. Jarmon's admonition that each of my childhood ghosts would need to be faced in order fully to be rid of them, not knowing exactly how many there would be at the onset.

One of the odd things that had flashed in my head during our last session as he delivered that prognosis was that I would need another 69 sessions to deal with all of the abuse events. (And yes, I am aware of the implication that number possesses, which adds to the weirdness!) Dr. Jarmon had no idea how many there would be and said so quite emphatically. And I don't know where that number came from but it was as lucid a recollection as the date of my birth, my phone number, my street address, or any other number that sits in my memory banks just waiting to be retrieved when needed. I didn't think about it; the number 69 just came flowing out.

I hadn't come to any conclusion before this second visit, but I was definitely questioning what real value would come from such a long-term exercise. I had validated the incest as a component of my childhood so what more did I need to know? In truth, I was far more interested in the implications of reincarnation as a precursor to this childhood after the previous revelations. That had now become my primary motivation. As I mentioned earlier, except for a weight problem, my general health and life were quite wonderful and normal. I didn't see what would be accomplished by spending years in therapy – a decision for another day.

As would be the pattern for our sessions, we began by talking about my previous visit and how I had absorbed the information. I confided my reluctance to accept what I had experienced under hypnosis, but in the end, the experience was so profoundly real and persuasive, there was nothing to do but accept the truth of it. The paradox was the most perplexing element for me. My conscious memory of my father was so utterly void of traits that I considered capable of doing what he did to me. And I was quite certain that no one who knew my father would believe me. So it was probably just as well that he had been dead for more than five years and there would not be any sort of confrontation that would set up an ugly "he said" "she said" dialogue.

The hypnotic state came again without effort. This time, Dr. Jarmon urged me to return to my childhood, which evolved into a very detailed memory of me at the age of about two, two and a half.

It's a sunny, warm day. I am in a play dress, outside in the yard, squatting and extremely curious about everything in the dirt. I stroke the ground with a fallen twig, looking for nothing in particular, but happy to be outside and exploring for hidden treasures.

I am finally attracted to a caterpillar that is finding its way ever so patiently across my view. I reach to pick it up. Missed! Again I grab. Again I miss. I finally settle into petting it – until it morphs into my father's penis. I am furious at the intrusion into my play, but I am not being consulted.

My father grabs me under my arms and lifts me into the air above his supine body, settling me on top of his erect penis so that I feel him in my crotch. He bounces me for awhile until he is limp, at which time he sets me aside to return to my play. He dozes for a short time, eyes closed and quite peaceful to look at. I walk away and sit down in the dirt and grab for the brown liquid, watching it run through my stubby fingers.

Dr. Jarmon asked me at this pause in my hypnotic story, whether or not my father had admonished me not to tell anyone about our play. My response was immediate and resigned. "He doesn't have to say anything. I know I'm not supposed to say anything to anyone." But I added with foreboding: "Mommy is going to be mad at me for getting my dress dirty."

As a two-year-old child, which my adult experience recognizes as a developing linguist with limited vocabulary and knowledge of the world, I already knew that this play my father and I were doing, was unspeakable and that I would get in trouble for dirtying my dress, while my father would escape even a mild inquisition. In the inimitable words of the Little Lady of *Three Men and a Little Lady* fame: WHAT A CROCK!

But my session was not over, and the transition into another memory was not progressing well. My mind was making all sorts of excuses: I was sure the session was almost up. I seriously considered bringing myself out of the hypnotic state. But my aware self prevailed, assuring me that Dr. Jarmon was quite capable of watching the clock. I instinctively didn't want to see what was coming next.

After I settled back into a deeper hypnotic state, acquiescing to my aware self, I was taken back to my bedroom where I was in a baby crib. I concluded that I was only about 5 months old. I was on my stomach sleeping and peaceful, which made it seem surprising that my father was leaning over the crib to pick me up. My tears well, my emotions go ballistic as I witness the unfolding scene.

My father has awakened me from sleep and is inserting his middle finger up my vagina. He proceeds to make a rattle of me, all the while balancing me with his other hand until the vibrating intrusion is concluded. God what a painful memory! How could anyone do that to a baby? How could my father do that to me? What had I done? I was sleeping peacefully. I did nothing to warrant this invasive assault. I was confused and extremely hurt recalling this incident.

Dr. Jarmon gently extracted me from the memory and directed me to rest. It was over. It was only a memory. I could not be hurt by it anymore. He continued his therapeutic monologue, bringing me out of the hypnosis with words of comfort and counsel.

One of the interesting things to me is the perspective of this memory. I am out of my body witnessing this from the perspective of an observer. Unlike the previous session's body memory experience, this was not a memory I felt, although the emotional toll was overwhelming. This experience is one that I observed under hypnosis.

My subsequent research into incest revealed that in very young children, the spirit often leaves the body under this sort of abuse, which would explain my ability to recall what was going on. In other contexts, such as near death experiences (NDEs), out-of-body experiences carry the full weight of details and emotion as in-body ones do.

It was also interesting to me that under hypnosis, I was genuinely curious about the caterpillar and the liquid dirt. I felt a child-like inquisitive spirit under hypnosis that was unexpected, but added validation and richness to the experience.

We have a wonderful set of survival mechanisms. I had optimistically (as I am wont to do on all matters) imagined an isolated occurrence of abuse that a session or two with Dr. Jarmon would resolve, and I would get on with the rest of my life. Here, in two sessions, was a sampling of abuse that my conscious mind could not even imagine, stretching from the crib into elementary school.

I am also curious about the meaning of all this juxtaposed against the very real and vivid conscious memory of a loving, gentle, religious/spiritual father. Blessings are taking on an entirely new and complex perspective.

# BATTLEFIELD

May 21 was a relatively normal session with Dr. Jarmon. What was significant was not a specific lifetime, but an emotional unworthiness that I was completely oblivious to on a conscious level.

The hypnotic state was invoked in the usual way. The process always included times for reflection and rest while still in the hypnotic state, and I was once again invited to spend some time on my safe, warm island in my imagination. I was then encouraged to experience what my aware self believed I was ready to see.

Surprisingly, for what must have been 30 to 40 minutes, I was surrounded by nothingness. Whereas my previous sessions had been quite visual – I had had clear images, colors and feelings presented to me – this experience was very black. I occasionally would feel and see what seemed like flashes of light. They would come and go. But no scenes, no emotions materialized. I was feeling frustrated that nothing was turning up, but at the same time feeling fully hypnotized and in an altered state of consciousness. I specifically remember hearing my aware self cajole: "Be patient. This will take some time." So I relaxed more, but still no visions were at hand. The only fleeting thought was that I was on a battle field: that the flashing lights were explosions and cannon fire. Dr. Jarmon, recognizing the time, and lack of experience, began to return me to my consciousness.

He again invited me to my safe and private island. But the strangest thing happened. I was overcome with a sense of unworthiness: I did not *deserve* to go to my island and rest. I have never in my conscious memory felt so unworthy. I was so ashamed of something: I was physically distressed when Dr. Jarmon had completed my return trip to his office.

Intellectually, it did not make sense. But I reasoned that I must have done something really appalling that I was having a hard time facing. I made a decision to try during my next appointment to spend as much of the session time under hypnosis as possible, to be patient with my aware self, and to understand just what was so terrible that I couldn't face.

The night before my appointment, I was reading Mia Parrow's book on codependence and read that some of our most difficult memories are buried in "black holes" to hide them and protect us. It sounded coincidently similar to the memory of my last appointment with Dr. Jarmon – the nothingness of my vision, and the utter sense of unworthiness that was totally foreign to me in my conscious existence. I made a mental note.

Events at the office conspired to force a cancellation of my next trip to New Jersey. It would be almost two months before I was again in Dr. Jarmon's comfy chair. But I had not forgotten about my earlier conviction to spend as much time under hypnosis as possible to try and understand the sense of unworthiness.

Dr. Jarmon accommodated me. After only a few minutes of preliminary how-are-you's we proceeded into the hypnosis. Again I basked in the sun on my private island: again I journeyed into my memory banks. This time my inner theater responded.

> I see myself marching along a hillside with a view of rolling hills and forests in the distance. The day is clear and beautiful. The sky is blue. I am a man. I am a soldier marching with my troops. I am not a person of official military rank, but I have the sense that I have some power in the group.

To his inquiry, I tell Dr. Jarmon that my name is Bill Smith. (I'm sure I'll have no problem finding that one in the National Archives!)

The setting is the American Civil War: and I am wearing a blue uniform and am relatively well dressed. We are marching at a comfortable pace: it's a beautiful day with no battle imminent. Dr. Jarmon directs me to go to the next scene.

I am sitting on the ground, with my back leaning against a large log. My knees are bent and slightly apart, my forearms are resting on my knee caps, and I am looking down at a dusty, but well-made pair of black leather boots. While I can tell I am staring at the ground, more importantly, I have my back turned away from something I don't care to witness.

"But you do know what's happening, don't you?" admonishes Dr. Jarmon. "Tell me what's going on."

There's a young boy who tags along with the troop.

"What's his name?"

I think his name is Joey. He helps us out. He fetches us water, gets whatever we may need. The sense is that he is what a squire might have been in King Arthur's day. He looks up to us: he worships us and wants to be just like us. And we're doing this to him.

"What are you doing?"

The men are gang raping him. He's being badly abused and I am sitting here, allowing it to happen. I could stop it, but I'm not. I know the men have done battle today and are crazy with fatigue; crazy with the war. But this is no way to treat a human being, I don't care what the circumstances. But I sit here, unable to come to his aid.

"What happens next?"

The men finish. It's quiet. I go to Joey to try to give him comfort; to help him out.

"Look into his eyes – they are the window to the soul. Do you see anyone you recognize?"

The identification sent shock waves throughout my body. I can still see those dark, desperate eyes, looking at me for answers, trying to understand the betrayal.

It's Deborah, my work colleague. I gasped as tears and disbelief flooded my entire being.

"What happens next?"

Morning comes. I am looking for Joey. I can't find him. I hope that he has run away – but I fear that he is dead. I think that I know that he is dead. I just hope that he ran away to salve my conscience.

"What do you do after the war?"

I see myself in a suit – a brown tweed suit with a vest. I am portly and sitting at a roll top desk, probably some sort of bureaucrat or accountant. I sense that I am hiding away in a safe place, so no one will ask me about my "war crimes." The only real concern I have is for the Joey incident – not anything I did on the battle field.

"Go to the end of this lifetime. What do you see?"

I die alone. No one is at my funeral, although I have a relatively nice casket. I sense that because I am a veteran, the government is giving me a burial. But I never married, and do not have any friends or relatives in attendance.

"And what did you learn from this lifetime?"

The overwhelming sense is the shame of not intervening to protect and save Joey; turning my back on another human being; of allowing it to happen. This is not the way to treat ANY human being, regardless of the circumstances; war or no war.

Dr. Jarmon eases me out of this memory with his soothing words and acknowledgement that this experience is over. He invites my aware self to show me more. I am still under hypnosis.

I am a woman riding in a fine, horse-drawn carriage, dressed in a full-length dress with jacket and matching hat, traveling to visit friends in a well-to-do part of the city. It appears to be France and Paris, possibly. It feels like the era of the *Tale of Two Cities* (mid-18th century). This is a social call, but not strictly a domestic call: it feels like we are participants in some sort of political cause. My name is Marie. I do not know the names of the women I am going to see. But as I ascend the steps of the row-house, I am greeted by the souls of two of my present-day friends.

Under hypnosis, I experience a great sense of joy that these women are known to me in this lifetime. I am delighted at the memory.

We greet each other with the usual chit-chat. We are in the home of one of these women – I don't have a strong sense whose home it is. We eventually settle in the parlor where I am distracted by my personal thoughts. I believe that we are discussing something of relative political significance, but I am distracted by the presence of the daughter of the woman in whose home we are meeting. She is poorly clothed and her demeanor is exceptionally submissive. I am immediately appalled by her status in her own home. I am aware that there is a son who wants for nothing in clothing, freedom or regard by his parents. But this daughter is being treated like a slave in her own home.

Appalled as I am, I say nothing: I am reluctant to insult my friend. But this too, is not the way to treat any human being. There is no lack of money in the family: no inability to treat this child in a manner similar to her brother. There is only the choice of my friend to continue this treatment, for reasons that I have no understanding of, even under hypnosis.

Again, I turn my back on the situation and condone this treatment by my silence. It's none of my business. I am even somewhat reluctant to understand under hypnosis, which of my friends, in this lifetime, is the mother. But of the two soul friends, one in this lifetime is a black woman, and I wonder if there might be a karmic connection for her to this lifetime in France, where she discriminated between her own children, and her current choice of soul experience?

Likely owing to the session time, Dr. Jarmon brought me back to my current reality without asking his usual "What did you learn in this lifetime?" question. Had he, I think my response would have been: The conspiracy of silence has deep, deep roots.

# THREE BOXES

I again journeyed to Spring Lake. Dr. Jarmon asked the usual questions: What did I want to accomplish today? Had I had any new thoughts or questions since last time?

I had begun to read *The Courage to Heal* in earnest since my last visit. I was not too excited about the opinion presented by the authors that years and years of time were needed to resolve all of this early abuse. I had to admit though, that I felt very blessed that I had not had to deal with drug or alcohol addiction, self mutilation, or other forms of self destruction that so many women in my circumstances have dealt with. Compared to the stories related in *The Courage to Heal*, I had been very fortunate: I was in really good shape.

I was in the shower one morning, feeling especially blessed, when I asked my aware self why I had not had to experience those sorts of problems as a result of the abuse? In jest, and with a slight German accent, she responded: "Ve haf other plans for you!" OK!? I was taken aback somewhat by the accent, but I knew I would find out sooner or later.

I was responding to the hypnosis more quickly than my previous visits. I could feel the altered consciousness and relaxation taking hold. But even though I knew I was under, I was not having any spontaneous images. Dr. Jarmon grasped the impasse: he gave me a riddle to help direct my experience.

"Imagine that you have three boxes in front of you on the ground. They are about the size of shoe boxes. The first contains clues about the origin of your problem, The second contains clues about how the problem is manifesting itself in this lifetime. The third has clues about what you need to do about this problem to get past it and move on." That little nudge was all I needed to get started.

> I opened the lid of the first box, and as I was peering inside, out came a horse, very much like the enhanced image EXXON used at one time in its commercial, where a car morphs into a roaring tiger. At the end of this transition, I was in the presence of a full-sized horse. I knew it was my horse. I grabbed its mane, swung up on its back and galloped away in great pleasure across the rolling hills and green grass. I experienced a very wonderful feeling – carefree and thrilling. I am a Native American, a boy, about 10 years old, bare-chested and bare-legged. I ride with the wind in my face, having the time of my life.

(In an earlier chapter of our life together, my husband and I owned five horses and a small farm. My most cherished fantasy about those horses was learning to ride well enough someday and be able to find space to just ride my horse at a gentle gallop across grassy lands, with absolutely no purpose in mind. I had no desire to ride in shows, to do English or Western riding for example. I just wanted to ride with the wind in my face across the land.)

I described what I was doing. Dr. Jarmon didn't let me ride in my carefree state too long – we had work to do. "What is happening in the next scene?"

> I am being summoned to my grandfather's lodge by one of the older boys in the tribe. There is urgency in his voice. It is obvious to me that I must go to the boy calling me and see if I can help. Something really must be wrong.

"Who is calling you? Does he call you by name? What is your name?"

> No, I do not sense my name. I do not know his. But I have a

scary feeling that something is very wrong with my grandfather – maybe he is dying. The boy calling me is 15 - 16 years of age. As soon as I arrive, he lifts the flap of the lodge and ushers me in. My grandfather is a wise man; an elder in the tribe. I don't know whether he is a medicine man, or just a very wise man. He is highly respected by the tribe, and given a great deal of reverence and honor. I am proud that I am his grandson. But as I look around and see no one dying, just my grandfather lying down on the floor of the lodge, I am having a hard time understanding why I have been called to his side with such urgency.

My grandfather is wearing very beautiful beads all over his chest. They are laced together and form a sort of tunic that covers two thirds of his chest. There are feathers and other ornamental things on it: it is very colorful. It is a prized possession and a status symbol in our tribe.

I become very silent and pensive.

Dr. Jarmon inquires against my silence. "What is your grandfather doing? What are you doing?"

I am very reluctant to tell him what is going on. I don't believe what I am feeling. I am overcome with waves of emotion. I attempt to hold back the message, not believing what I am hearing. This can't be the reason I was so urgently summoned away from my play. But now, the tears and the anger well up and I continue my dialog through a flood of tears. He's forcing me to put his penis in my mouth. He is holding my head down. I can feel his penis in my mouth, and it is very upsetting.

Dr. Jarmon helps me through the memory, but I am not easily calmed.

I am very upset that this is happening to me. I didn't do anything to deserve this treatment! No one warned me about this happening. This is the last person I would expect to treat me like this. Why is he doing this to me?

As the experience becomes less intense and I am relieved of the anger and disgust through Dr. Jarmon's counsel, he suggests that I go on to another scene. But I insist on editorializing. The events of my story are telling. Much more was happening on an emotional level.

What is so repugnant about this experience is not the oral sex, per se, but rather the false pretenses under which I was lured to my grandfather's lodge. I genuinely believed that something was wrong. I was innocently going to try and help – bring comfort if I could. And this indignity was the thanks for my concern. It didn't feel like sex. It felt like a **conspiracy**.

"Was the boy using you so he wouldn't have to do it?"

No. There did not seem to be a sense of "Better you than me." My grandfather wanted the younger boys. It feels like this is some sort of perverted initiation rite: a passage into some sort of tribal society – an unspoken society of the men and boys in the tribe.

"Do you recognize any of the souls from this life time?"

Yes. I was aghast. My grandfather is my father in this lifetime and the 16 year-old boy who lured me to the original encounter, is my mother in my present life.

"At some point, your grandfather dies. Can you relate what is happening at that time?"

Yes. I am about 30. I have a young son, about five or six. I am standing with my arm on my young son's shoulder, watching my grandfather be cremated on a ceremonial funeral pyre. He is wearing the same beaded tunic that I remember him wearing the first time he violated me. He is being sent to the spirit world with great honor and respect. This ceremony is not for a common person. It is reserved only for the wisest and most respected members of the tribe.

"And how do you feel?"

I'm glad the bastard is dead! I am glad that he will not be able to do to my son what he did to me. I am also disgusted with the mockery of the entire affair. I am not the only one in the tribe to have been exploited by him. But everyone is pretending that

this was a great man, deserving of our love and respect.
"What did you learn from this life?"

I learned what a conspiracy is: that silence can serve a very sick purpose. If cruel secrets and using people for selfish intentions are unspoken, we can pretend that they don't exist, but the pretense is hollow. We all know the truth and the implications. We're just not willing to say anything and in return, the injustice persists.

"Let's go back to the second box. What do you find in there?"

There is a bauble inside that I can't give a name to: it's like nothing I've ever seen. It is V-shaped. It seems to have one feathery prong, and one solid side. Maybe it's an ornament of some sort. There seems to be a hinge where the two sides meet. But it doesn't have a name: it doesn't seem to have any purpose. I haven't the faintest idea what it is. I can't imagine what this has to do with my current circumstances.

"What happens when you unhinge it?"

The object was immediately recognizable to me, but I did not want to tell Dr. Jarmon. I remained silent. My entire body was trembling with a message I did not want to hear.

"Let's go on to the third box. This one contains clues about what you need to do to get through this in this life time."

I reluctantly began to let Dr. Jarmon in on my discovery. I was already in the third box, when he guided me to the second.

I had already been able to analyze the meaning of this bauble and I was scared to death about the implications. This was a private matter, and I wanted to deal with it privately. I hadn't wanted to tell anyone about my circumstances – that's why I had driven four hours to New Jersey so as not to chance a run-in with someone I knew.

The bauble is a quill – a writing quill.

"Put it in your hand. Write with it. What are you writing?"

The words came swiftly, and without hesitation. The message was causing untold physical reactions in the core of my body. I was again reluctant to tell Dr. Jarmon.

"What are you writing?"

It's Time to End the Conspiracy.

Dr. Jarmon allowed that my aware self might have other things to show me and directed her to proceed. I was stuck on this assignment however, and my mind was racing forward. I knew that I could exit the hypnosis if I wanted to, but I gently admonished myself that that was probably unwise. But my silence did not go unnoticed by Dr. Jarmon, who soon recognized my state, and brought me back.

Am I supposed to write a book about this?

"Sounds pretty clear to me."

That's really bizarre. A few days ago, while I was lying in bed, waiting for my husband to finish his morning shower, Rush Limbaugh gave his usual three-minute "thought for the day" on my morning news radio station, which irked me no end. He was pontificating about how relationships *should* operate. But without conscious intent, my mind's eye immediately flashed on a book, with a black cover, and the words FAMILY VALUES yelling from the book jacket. It had a subtitle "The Way Things ARE" in defiance of Limbaugh's preaching monologue about the way things ought to be.

The subtitle was wrong. It is supposed to be: It's Time to End the Conspiracy.

## FAMILY VALUES
### It's Time to End the Conspiracy

"A lot to think about."

I don't know if I can handle this. I've never written a book. I don't know if I can bare my soul like this. It's scary. It's really, really scary. But it feels like I just got an assignment.

"You only need to look inside. There you will find all the material you'll need."

# TEMPLE JOB

I never returned to Spring Lake – not for anything Dr. Jarmon had done or didn't do – life has a way of morphing. I had faced more than enough thought-provoking events to engage me, as a result of the four sessions in six months that I had traveled to New Jersey to experience.

I too was morphing. My immediate sense of liking the concept of reincarnation and my running head-first into its bosom propelled me to read and investigate more. And there was also a gradual internalization of the concept. I started paying more attention to what I was doing, and spent less time worrying about what other people were doing. I became more critical of the way I was acting and reacting to life: I reflected that if others continued to act in ways that I found disturbing, my righteous indignation waned with the belief that they were in charge of their own karma – not me – and would have to deal with it themselves some day. For me, the implications of reincarnation were very emancipating.

It also was a tonic for victimization. I couldn't feel sorry for myself, incest or not, even though incest is utterly repugnant and needs to be expunged from our culture in all its insidious forms. (Fortunately we no longer offer up human sacrifices to the gods, so maybe incest will someday be a thing of the past too.) And if I considered the more holistic picture of my lifetimes, I had not been an innocent bystander. I had to look at how I was contributing to my circumstances: what lessons I was learning and what responses would contribute to my soul's growth and my ability to learn planet-earth's lessons once and for all. And in the most paradoxical way imaginable, maybe my father was a loving contributor toward my soul's growth. Who can know?

I researched and found a therapist in my local area that did past life regressions and saw her on occasion to deal with personal questions concerning more general topics. I continued to be a member of the Association for Research and Enlightenment (ARE) and signed up for a conference one fall weekend in 1994 featuring Hazel M. Denning, Ph.D., who lived and worked in Riverside, California, and had spent more than 35 years doing past life regressions.

I came across Dr. Denning's work in my research and wrote to her before the conference, asking for a regression session in Virginia Beach. She was happy to oblige, however, it would have to be on Sunday after the conference concluded, as her agreement with ARE stipulated that she could not give any sessions during the course of the conference. I had no problem delaying my return to northern Virginia for an extra hour or so after the conference concluded, so we agreed to meet.

The conference was well attended and had excellent speakers in addition to Dr. Denning. However, late Sunday morning, there was a tap on my shoulder asking if I was Margaret McElrath. Yes. Please call home immediately.

When I contacted my husband, I learned that our youngest daughter had her appendix removed that morning at 7 a.m. and was in the hospital ICU recovering from a burst appendix that had languished and had already become gangrenous by the time they got her into surgery. The otherwise routine hour-long procedure had taken four and a half hours and while the operation was successful, my daughter would be on intravenous antibiotics for a week to ensure the most positive outcome. I was shaken by the news and seriously contemplated canceling my session with Dr. Denning to get home a little earlier, but there wasn't much I could do from a practical standpoint. My husband and the medical professionals had it all under control.

I ultimately decided to keep the appointment, but not without a significant amount of guilt accompanying that decision.

My session with Dr. Denning began with a synopsis of everything that I had done over the previous couple of years, and what I hoped to accomplish. I don't recall that I had any specific subject to cover. I still was just not thoroughly comfortable with everything I had learned. I was certain there was more, and hoped she could help me go further into my past.

The hypnotic state was not happening as seamlessly as I had hoped. I know the pangs of guilt and worry I harbored were contributing to my retarded progress. But eventually I was in an altered consciousness responding to Dr. Denning's guidance.

"Look at your feet. What are you wearing?"

I have on sandals and am wearing a white garment, probably some sort of toga, but there's not as much fabric as I'd expect a toga to have; no fabric flung over my shoulder, for example.

"What century do you think you're in?"

This seems to be pre-Christian times, but not Egypt. It feels like I'm living in a very large city.

"What country are you in?"

I sense I am somewhere in the Mediterranean area. Rome maybe? It's very warm and sunny and this seems to be the normal state of the climate.

"Where are you just now?"

I'm standing on a massive staircase into a temple of some sort. It's all marble and stone. There are massive columns and a butterfly carved into the stone over the entrance. It's a very imposing façade and very prominent in the skyline: it sits on a hill.

"Who's inside?"

I'm stunned to see Dr. Jarmon, Dr. Weiss, and Dr. Denning sitting around a table having a meal, but reveal nothing of this to Dr. Denning. On one level, I'm convinced I am making this up and not really having an authentic experience. Just as that original hypnotic session with my uncle Duke, I'm aware of a

split sort of consciousness; one sharing what I'm experiencing
at an altered-consciousness level, and another cognizant of the
Sunday afternoon reality of my daughter in the hospital. I
consider throwing in the towel and bringing myself out of the
state, when Dr. Denning, sensing an impasse, prompts me with
another question.

"Are you coming or going?"

That question stopped me in my tracks.

I'm leaving – was my immediate, uncalculated response.

And my conflict about terminating the session and going back to
northern Virginia to see my daughter was resolved once and for all.

I see myself with my back to the church, walking down the
steps, away from the entrance.

The impact of me witnessing myself turning my back on the
temple, aligned incredibly with the two lifetimes uncovered with Dr.
Jarmon and added a sense of credibility to the session that allowed me
to stay in my altered state, allowing more information to come forward.

I have turned my back on the church and will never be
returning. I don't know what I will do or where I will go, but I
am leaving for good. I will never come back!

"Why are you leaving? What happened in the temple?"

I am a priest, and my job is to castrate young boys to be
eunuchs for the church. I can't do this anymore. This is not the
way to treat children. This can't be what God intended.

Beyond this brief statement, I am not articulating anything to Dr.
Denning, but under hypnosis, I know that I have a very comfortable
living situation and by staying and continuing to perform my job, I'll be
set for the rest of my life. Leaving as I have chosen to do is going to be
difficult. I will have no income. I will have no peers to talk to and
befriend. This exit is not a spur-of-the-moment decision. I had given
the matter a great deal of thought and ultimately concluded that having
nothing was better than this "something."

"Go to the end of this lifetime. What are you doing?"

I am quite old and living in a very small, sparsely furnished room with a dirt floor. The house is white-washed, with thick walls, and openings for windows and a door, but nothing on the windows or door: a simple room, open to the elements. I lived the rest of my life here watching over the young boys as they played in the square. I was their self-appointed guardian, ensuring that they could play and grow up without having to be subjected to the sort of torture I had put so many like them through for the sake of the church. I die on the dirt floor apparently from natural causes, without any family or friends, curled up in the corner.

Dr. Denning invites me to relax and delivers the benediction of this being a past experience and one that will no longer affect me. She continues her monologue until I am returned to my normal consciousness.

I am struck by the full circle I have experienced. I shared with Dr. Denning that this last scene of my death on a dirt floor, had been my first regression experience more than three years ago in Virginia Beach, when I had first heard Dr. Weiss speak about *Many Lives, Many Masters*.

And over the next weeks and months, I would often think about this temple job. What life-limiting choices a young boy would be forced to make to serve the church – no marriage, no family, no career. And I can only imagine the pain and suffering I inflicted on countless young boys even if they survived the ordeal. This was before anesthesia and sanitation. And while I suppose the body would heal over time given no infection and a healthy body, I can also imagine that I may have killed young boys in the process. What if one had been a hemophiliac? He would certainly have died from losing blood during such a surgical procedure (and I have no concept of what sorts of surgical instruments I had). Without anesthesia, the procedure likely would have generated spine-chilling screams from pain and massive amounts of blood to deal with on a regular basis.

One of the remarkable outcomes of this memory was to relieve me of my aversion to needles and blood. As I related earlier in my story, I fainted as a child every time I got a polio shot and had to be supervised by the school principal. My ability to handle medical procedures on my children was pathetic. My loving husband always came to my aid and handled the ER visits and stitches. As a young woman I tried to give blood for the brother of a colleague who had been badly burned. However I went into shock and had to be rescued by an off-site hospital physician called to handle my condition. When I left several hours later, I was kindly asked never to give blood again.

My childhood memory of being taken to get immunization shots at the county clinic and distinctively hearing spine-chilling screams, took on new meaning after this regression. Like so many things associated with reincarnation, I have no clue how they work, but I can guess as well as the next person.

Somehow, the memory of my temple job and the spine-chilling screams that would have accompanied a castrating procedure, attached itself to medical needles and blood in this lifetime via the childhood experience of the visit to the clinic for immunization shots.

Dr. Denning promised that the temple-job lifetime would no longer affect me after the session, and true to her statement, the attachment was severed completely. I am now able to calmly endure routine blood tests, assist with minor cuts without fainting or feeling nauseous, and give blood, banking more than 30 pints at various blood drives since the session with Dr. Denning.

God truly does work in mysterious ways.

# REUNION

Before he died, my father let it be known to numerous like-minded family and friends, that if he had an opportunity to communicate from the other side he would do it. I recall my Aunt Lois attending a seminar not too long after Dad died and hearing the medium ask whether anyone knew "Uncle Bob." She remained silent but wondered aloud later whether this truly was Dad attempting to make contact, since he was known as Uncle Bob to our extended family – never Robert.

Reflecting on everything that had happened in the years following my epiphany, I was still attached to the idea about wanting to make contact with my father's spirit and ask some still-perplexing questions. I thought it would be exceptionally informative to hear from him where he would obviously have a different perspective.

You may recall that the weekend in Virginia Beach with Dr. Weiss and Dr. Jarmon included an impromptu lecture in the ARE Library by Dr. Raymond Moody, who had spent his career dealing with metaphysical ideas and spirit communications. He has documented hundreds of contacts, but the primary characteristic is that they are in response to a traumatic event such as getting struck by lightning, or via some sort of medium who acts as a go-between. The point of his lecture was to share his discoveries about how we might be able to create a situation where we could engage with the spirit world in a deliberate way and on a one-on-one basis, not through the gift of a medium.

In his research, Dr. Moody examined the writings of Herodotus, a 5th century BC Greek historian, who is known as the Father of History. Herodotus was the first historian to collect his materials systematically, test their accuracy, and arrange them in well constructed and vivid narratives.

One of Herodotus' treatises described the Oracle at Delphi and recorded that all manner of people would traverse a labyrinth underground, first to be stripped of their worldly orientation, and subsequently to engage in communications with deceased entities. Dr. Moody reflected that it is interesting that Herodotus is credited with writing down accurate accounts of history, but this particular account is routinely discounted by many if not most, since we know perfectly well that you cannot converse with spirits.

But Dr. Moody was intrigued, and after additional research and visits to Greece and the Oracle at Delphi, has replicated in his "Theatre of the Mind" in rural Alabama, a labyrinth and protocol to replicate the experience of the Oracle and allow people to communicate with spirits in another dimension. His book *Reunions*, published in 1993 describes his research, the protocol for reunions, and stories of individuals successfully communicating with deceased loved ones.

*Reunions* gave me the impetus to contact Dr. Moody's Theatre of the Mind and make an appointment. What did I have to lose?

TWA's flight 737 traveled from National Airport, Washington, D.C., to Atlanta, Georgia, and carried me to what I considered a milestone in my personal journey. My appointment with Dr. Moody was scheduled for Sunday at 10:00 AM. I anticipated a reunion with my father who died a little over six years before.

Prior to my trip, my friend and colleague Deborah, who was aware of my plans, called and related that she had happened to tune into a radio talk show and was startled by the notion that spirits might want to contact us as eagerly as we may want to contact them.

The talk show medium helped a grieving widow who not only lost her husband recently, but also had lost her two sons 14 years prior. The sons had been trying to contact their mother in any way that they could. They would cause the phone to ring: the light bulbs in the house were constantly going out (more so than would normally be expected). These things the medium related before the grieving woman ever gave the medium her name. The information proved to be a great relief to her.

I too felt that this meeting with Dr. Moody was a combination of my desire to contact my father and his desire to contact me. As my sessions with Dr. Jarmon have demonstrated, my father and I have had a long history together.

As usual, I was running late. I had hoped to leave the house by 9:45 am to give me ample time to catch my 11:45 am flight. As usual, it was later, almost 10:00 am before I left the house.

National airport is 20-25 miles away. It being a Saturday morning, there was no rush-hour traffic, but there was moderate traffic. Regardless, I sailed through to Alexandria without a hiccup. I arrived about 10:30 and parked my car in the long-term lot. From there I took a shuttle bus – which just happened to be sitting, waiting for me. As soon as I stepped on board, he drove me to the terminal. The time was about 10:45 am. At the terminal there was a line at the TWA counter, so I walked back outside to the curb-side baggage handler who had no customers, dropped my bag and headed for the departure gate. After checking in, I sat down for no more than a couple of minutes before the plane boarded. I had a window seat and an empty bank of seats next to me. After I finished my journal entry, I had a brief but delightful conversation with a 6-year old.

Before we arrived, I had a conversation with myself about the daily rate I got through the travel agent on my Alamo car. It was $46.98 per day. That seemed a bit high for a weekend, but it was supposed to be the cheapest rate the Travelogue person could find. I promised myself that I would ask before I signed the contract.

When we arrived at the terminal, lines at Hertz, Avis, Dollar and

National were 10-15 people deep. I didn't even see Alamo at first.

I found the baggage turnstile, but the bags from our flight were nowhere in sight. I decided to try and find the Alamo counter and take care of the rental business before I retrieved my bag. The line at Alamo was no better. In fact Alamo looked to have a line twice the length of the Avis & Hertz lines. At Budget, there was no one – only the counter person! I asked the daily rate: $35 for a mid-sized car, unlimited mileage. I would save $12 a day and not have to wait in a queue! Someone was looking out for me.

I was directed around the corner to the car rental shuttle stops. Here too, was the Budget shuttle just waiting for someone. I got on board and was whisked away to the car lot. Door to door, my day flowed unchallenged – no stops or faltering along the way. But the icing on the cake was the music that was playing on the shuttle as it drove away from the airport. It choked me up and brought tears to my eyes. I knew the song, but I didn't remember hearing it for a very long time. I sang the familiar words, as the tune became infectious.

> More than the greatest love the world has known
> This is the love I give to you alone
> More than the simple words I try to say
> I only live to love you more each day.
> More than you'll ever know
> My arms long to hold you so
> My life will be in your keeping
> Waking, sleeping, laughing, weeping.
> Longer than always is a long, long time
> But far beyond forever, you'll be mine
> I know I've never lived before, and my heart is very sure
> No one else could love you more!

I felt as though my father had synchronized these events, and was welcoming me to Atlanta with love. I took it as a good omen.

I arrived at the B&B in Alabama I would call home for a couple of days in mid-afternoon, having crossed the central time zone and gained an hour in the process. I spent the afternoon shopping and treated myself to a wonderful meal. As I laid back to reflect on the day and what might happen tomorrow, I made note of the flawless logistics that had brought me here. If I read the signs correctly, this trip was certainly meant to happen!

I awoke without an alarm. The morning was gentle and peaceful. I had a light breakfast as prescribed – Apple-Cinnamon herbal tea instead of coffee. I took time to read a portion of the Sunday newspaper from the sunlit, greenhouse porch surrounding the front of the B&B.

I arrived at the agreed location a few minutes early and was greeted by three of Dr. Moody's assistants. They welcomed me and began their orientation to the Theatre. I had initially expected to be greeted by Dr. Moody, and initially assumed he would be guiding me through the experience personally. But he was in Colorado on business.

I was stunned and devastated! I totally lost my bearings when I realized Dr. Moody would not be assisting me with my reunion. The euphoria of my flight and the flawless logistics turned into a knot in my stomach and a feeling of betrayal that lasted days. In retrospect, no one had promised that Dr. Moody would be present: I just assumed it. And although I completed the orientation with the staff and spent the allotted 45 minutes in the Theatre, my mind was elsewhere and the reunion, non-existent.

I was having a very stressful conversation in my head about the situation, and couldn't shut it off. I vacillated between feeling manipulated and deceived by the Theatre staff and disgusted with myself for making assumptions that had nothing to do with the purpose of my visit. The result was a complete failure to communicate with my father and validate the pledge that we could communicate with the deceased. The staff recognized my disorientation – although I never confided the true source of my discontent – and tried in vain to counsel me and help me through my predicament, but it was not to be.

Profoundly disappointed and frustrated with my reaction to Dr. Moody's absence, I returned to the B&B and picked up *A Course in Miracles*, which I had brought with me and opened immediately to these words:

> Any split in mind must involve a rejection of part of it, and this is the belief in separation. The wholeness of God, which is His peace, cannot be appreciated except by a whole mind that recognizes the wholeness of God's creation. By this recognition it knows its creator. ***Exclusion and separation are synonymous*** (emphasis mine) as are separation and dissociation and that once it occurs projection becomes its main defense or the device that keeps it going. The reason, however, may not be so obvious as you think.
>
> What you project, you disown, and therefore do not believe is yours. ***You are excluding yourself by the very judgment that you are different from the one on whom you project*** (emphasis mine). Since you have also judged against what you project, you continue to attack it because you continue to keep it separated.

If the truth be known, although that evening I understood the words the *Course* was sharing, it took me several days to fully appreciate the implications and how *I* had created my failure to communicate with my father. I finally realized that unbeknownst to me on a conscious level, I had projected my innate value and power in the situation to Dr. Moody. I had sabotaged my experience by subconsciously deciding that I was not capable *on my own* to accomplish what his research indicated was possible: somehow I had to be in Dr. Moody's presence for the reunion to materialize. Although I had accepted the premise of his ideas, I had projected their efficacy onto the human being who voiced them – not the validity and truthfulness of the idea – an all too common human response I would suggest, to all manner of ideas and circumstances.

And then, failing to have the experience I had paid to have, I immediately found fault with Dr. Moody, his staff, and the Theatre; not very fair or self-aware. I thought I had come pretty far in my spiritual journey, but here was ample evidence that I still had lots of work to do, and self love to embrace.

I reflected on this disappointing outcome for several weeks, and ultimately gave myself a little slack. We are conditioned and socialized from the moment we arrive on the planet, to conform to what others have determined is in our best interests. And often the conditioning is loving and benign.

But when abuse is present, fear robs us of our innate, God-given power, teaching us that our needs are not as important as those of our abuser. We are second-class citizens and the conditioning becomes more and more ingrained as the years accumulate and we are reminded again and again via cultural norms that someone else (teacher, preacher, celebrity, spouse, boss, etc.) is somehow more important than we are. Society reveres authority figures and we create laws and mores to buttress their ability to thrive, whether they are benevolent leaders or bullies or worse. We create belief and organizational hierarchies that belie any real sense of equality. So separation and inequality become legitimized. And we develop mechanisms to cope, some strategies more supportive of our well-being than others.

And besides abuse teaching inequality, it also ingrains fear, especially when the abused looks to the abuser for protection, sustenance and love for survival. Fear erodes trust and becomes a huge component of our coping mechanisms. We play it safe, hide when we feel threatened, justify suffering and fail to accomplish everything we are humanly capable of and for which, the gift of life was given. Fear that was intended to protect us from being mauled or eaten by other of God's creatures has evolved over the years into all manner of rationale for not embracing and creating love. Over millennia, it's become far more common – and commercially beneficial – to embrace and create fear as a basis for our human interactions.

My reaction at The Theatre of the Mind was fear-based, but it took the experience to call attention to that reality.

Fear is so insidious that it's become unrecognizable for what it is. It is so ingrained in our cultural norms that we've become blinded to its pervasive presence in our lives. But recognizing its insidious presence doesn't make it an easy reality to neutralize or change. The implications are actually quite mind-boggling!

# REFLECTIONS

The attempted reunion with my father, took place more than 20 years ago, so you might be wondering what I've been up to since. The ultimate truth is that I've been doing what every other human being does: live as best as can be expected under the circumstances. That said, the insights and effects of my epiphany probably give me a different perspective than most people share.

There is a Zen proverb that is also reflected in the title of one of the first books I ever read in the spiritual genre: **Chop Wood Carry Water**. I believe the complete proverb is: "Before enlightenment, chop wood, carry water. After enlightenment, chop wood, carry water." The difference (with enlightenment/education) is in what we bring to the chore, or more broadly, what we bring to our life. It's amazing in retrospect how much baggage we collect along the way in terms of beliefs and prejudices that have no bearing or purpose for our life, and we don't often recognize that we've picked them up and continue to burden ourselves with their weight.

Overarching is my belief that living today – this lifetime – is by far the most important activity I can undertake. I was given an extraordinary opportunity to more fully understand my situation – ask and you shall receive – but as some might admonish – be careful what you ask for. In truth, I am grateful for both perspectives. I am extremely grateful for the freedom to make the choices I've been able to make. But my experience does not embolden me to recommend that you follow in my footsteps.

My journey hasn't been without sadness and difficulties. I strained and lost relationships that were meaningful to me in the process and had to reframe others that were impacted by my epiphany. For while my father passed away before the incest came into my consciousness, my mother lived to remarry at 72 and remain earthbound until she was 90 years old, spending the last 10 years of her life in the murkiness of Alzheimer's. My brothers are supportive of my story, but I was saddened to learn that my older brother maintained a perspective and jealousy that I had monopolized all of Dad's time when we were children, which likely is a major reason that he and I didn't get along well growing up. It was difficult to hear, since I don't have a conscious memory of spending lots of time with my father, and I'm sure that meant that my brother was negatively impacted by growing up with a mostly-absent father. And based on the texts about incest, I have been concerned that my younger brother also may have been similarly abused: he shares traits with other survivors, and I have shared my concerns with him. Unfortunately, like other forms of abuse, incest creates collateral damage for many other lives when it touches them with neglect, fear, and denial.

But healing – and the appetite for seeking truth – is often elusive, and rarely supported by our normal daily activities and cultural norms. It is much easier to live in a world of denial and assert our omnipotence than embrace a more nuanced explanation for our ills and successes. Denial is an insidious refusal to see truth when it is staring you in the face. Living in denial dodges truth, often because it is too painful or complex to deal with.

My mother lived a significant portion of her life in denial, and although I am no medical researcher, I'm personally convinced that Mother's denial strategies to cope with the evidence of my abuse, contributed significantly to her Alzheimer's. But in fairness, *her* mother's experience with divorce in the early 1900's and subsequent admonition to her children never to divorce, set up a Catch-22 that limited her options. I am certain that survivors of domestic abuse can relate with my mother.

So what is a compassionate human being to do?

After the reunion debacle, I decided to try a more conventional approach to aid my healing. At a yoga class, I was introduced to Margaret, a licensed therapist, and spent over four years in her excellent counsel. I was fortunate to have medical insurance to cover the weekly expense, a luxury many survivors don't have access to I am sure. Talk therapy was our primary interaction, and I felt safe and heard in her home office, which was a completely new experience for me. Margaret was neither shocked nor alarmed by my thoughts, which often dealt with the relationship between my mother and me, more than any other relationship or event. She remarked one day that I had "grown myself up" which upon reflection seemed quite apt.

I was still highly functional in my profession, which primarily tapped into my left brain. Eventually I realized that what I still needed was to nurture and be nurtured. While attempting to cage the beast of my childhood and reincarnation, I realized that I had neglected my relationships with my husband and daughters. If I truly had come to the realization that it was in my best interests to live in the present and live *this* life, then I needed to get back to the daily act of living, and put the academic and somewhat distracting activities of my journey aside for awhile.

I stopped going to counseling, not because it wasn't helpful, but because if I honestly assessed the situation, I wanted Margaret to be my mother and have her in my life in that surrogate capacity. I knew that would never happen and my continued need for that relationship was directly impacting the more tangible and present relationships with my spouse and children. John never pried or reacted in a jealous way, but it was obvious he was anxious for my counseling to be finished. And so it was.

I remain in the mode of living every day to the best of my ability, seeking health and nurturing loving relationships wherever I can find them. I support my husband and children in the best ways I know how, sometimes listening when they need an ear, or hanging sheetrock for the library when that is the order of the day. I spend time in my garden and delight at the new buds and signs of life after a freezing winter. I take wood scraps, lawn clippings and trash to the dump on Jolly Pond Road. I luxuriate in the salon with color highlights and perms to enhance my fine, thin hair. I read novels that I had never thought I would be interested in. I waste time and don't always get things done. I play computer games more often than I probably should. I take heavy hors d'oeuvres to our community Mix and Mingle affairs. I visit Paris when the budget allows. I contribute to causes I can relate to and do 5Ks when the spirit moves me. I sleep like a baby. I go to the gym before breakfast whenever it makes sense. I see my doctors regularly and take my arthritis medicine. I have another book I want to write. I have fabric I want to design and nightgowns I want to sew.

I want to see tomorrow, and tomorrows 20 years from now with the same curiosity and joy I experience today. I want to learn from others who have expertise and experiences I have never encountered. And I know I will always find those with more knowledge, experience and talent than I possess. The perpetual student in me never worries about educational opportunities.

I want everyone on the planet to have loving companions and live a comfortable life without fear.

And there is no holy man, or guru, or politician, or medical doctor, or celebrity or institution or corporation that deserves an elevated status or my worship – the abdication of my equality. I will continue to seek truth, genius and relevance wherever I look and not wait for permission or anointment to proceed. I have a great deal of respect for dead and living human beings who show and educate us in what it means to be creative and human, and some empathy for the users whose delusional sense of entitlement creates hell on earth – they will meet their karma one day too.

I also know that my eternal soul doesn't need to take a backseat to anyone. I am no saint. I have my own set of idiosyncrasies and foibles that frustrate my family and friends. And if I am lucky, I will continue to grow and change and fine-tune this life until I take my last breath. I will forever be a work-in-progress.

I am at peace. I am content. I am finally comfortable in my own skin and enjoy planning for the future with attention and gratitude for what gets thrown in my path today.

Margaret McElrath

# IT'S ALL ABOUT LOVE

I subscribe to the spiritual tenet that declares we are created in the image of God. And if God is the Creator, then we too are creators – at least creators-in-training – and I would suggest that planet earth is our creative research and development lab. God is also Love, and his gift of free will through multiple lifetimes, allows us to create and experience the results of our creations, ultimately to learn that unconditional love is the only principle that delivers everlasting results. We ultimately come to realize what God-Love is all about.

I doubt that I would get any argument that God created the universe, our earth, and every species of vegetation and animal life on the planet. What we call nature, is God's creation.

I will assert, therefore, that anything that is not of nature is human-made and not God-made. And what is human-made, can be un-made or re-made if we are so inclined.

In addition to the physics and geography of our planet, our ideas have codified into beliefs whose context is a dominant contributor to our creative endeavors. The composite of human ideas and creations is where human culture is today. What we see on the news, what we experience in our family settings, and what we spend our time and energy on, all represent the sum total of our ideas, beliefs, and creative activities over millennia, and those we value and repeat over time, culture by culture.

At one juncture, it was common knowledge that the earth was flat. That popular notion did not make it so. But for centuries, the sun circled the earth and men were put to death for suggesting otherwise. We did not know enough at that time to accept that a spherical earth circling the sun might result in more opportunities for adventure and creative endeavors than the narrower concept of a flat earth. Curiosity and resulting knowledge ushered in a different way of relating the sun to the earth, although neither sun nor planet had moved: we just changed our perspective and created even more ideas and creative adventures.

I don't for a minute believe that humanity is focused on an end-game that's already been defined. I like Neale Donald Walsh's assertion that we are "God experiencing himself." As children of a creative force, we are creating what we are capable of creating in the context of planet earth. Stone Age man could not have created plumbing. The Romans could not have developed an electric blanket. And for all of our sophistication and space travel, we still don't know how to create world peace.

As human societies have evolved, innumerable creations have resulted. We created language. We created tools. We created money. We created education. We created science. We created laws. We created music. We created philosophy. We created culture. We created religions. We created banking institutions. We created fabrics. We created baseball. We created cars. We created governments. We created cities. We created resorts. We created airplanes. We created cement. We created computers. We created hot dogs. We created solar panels.

Our creations become more sophisticated and complex as our accumulated knowledge matures about how nature and physics work together to create new things. And somehow miraculously, they are married to our ideas, dreams, inspirations, and practical needs.

We have also created things that destroy what we have created, which seems counterintuitive.

We created the word enemy. We created weapons. We created

war. We created refugees. We created greed. We created them and us. We created all manner of words, belief structures, and social hierarchies to separate us and create polarizing results. We created right and wrong.

Yes, we created right and wrong. Right and wrong do not exist in nature. They are human-made concepts that continue to polarize us, promote *conditional* love, and limit our ability to establish peace on earth.

And I think right and wrong somehow evolved in our attempt to conjugate and manipulate love. I won't be the last in a very long list of people who point to *unconditional* love as the only sort of love that really matters. But for whatever reason, we seem to want to tip the scales away from that reality and give ourselves a special edge. I think it has a great deal to do with the knowledge of how to manipulate ideas for commercial gain – the money god. And over time we have chosen to add condition upon condition to satisfy other agendas, special interests and our sense that we are unique and superior to some other group of human beings, and deserve more of the planet's resources as a reward for our exceptionalism.

Creating right and wrong minimized our need to think about love. If it's "right" then we don't have to do the mind work of asking is it love? And if it's "wrong" then we *know* it's not love and something we should reject. We further conjugated love to ethical and unethical bifurcations, and legal and illegal ones with the same intent. We have molded love to suit various objectives that may or may not reap the ultimate benefits we thought would accrue by making the process simpler by creating these labels.

Somewhere along the way, we decided that certain human beings were more special than others; more deserving of life, liberty and the pursuit of happiness. So we have created systems and belief structures that reward those special among us and ignore and discount others we deem inferior, based on myriad criteria: sex, skin color, language, geography, customs, religion, politics, labels-on-the-inside-of-our-clothes, etc.: Lazy Love!

And as a result, we've created a cultural phenomenon that never asks the question: Is this Love? Is it Loving? If the culture thinks something is right then we are spared the hard work of knowing that in fact it is unconditional love speaking and not special interests. And if those cultural conventions are strong enough, then we can be manipulated quite effectively with right answers never being questioned or re-evaluated. We have evolved into a culture that puts its trust in lazy love.

Over the centuries, we have become conditioned to see life from a fear-based perspective, not a love-based one, even though countless mystics and wise human beings have stressed the importance of unconditional love. Moreover, our short-term perspective on life being limited to 70 or 80 years, conditions us to fear death, and reinforce – by our personal and collective choices – a commercial explanation for life: the one with the most toys wins! And in support of that hypothesis, we have created a society that turns its back on unconditional love, justifying greed with economic theories, religion, and entitlement mindsets.

But if God took billions upon billions of years to create the universe and we were created in his image, how – and why – would He be finished with us after only 70 or 80 years?

The metaphysical perspective explains that we are souls having an earthly experience. Reincarnation is just part of the process. Simply stated, we experience through multiple earthly existences, the results and effects of our creative endeavors. If we create loving expressions, we experience loving results in another lifetime and get to create new things out of new technologies in another lifetime. And conversely, if we create eunuchs as servants for our church, we may experience child abuse in a subsequent lifetime to experience the effects of our choices in order fully to understand what we created and teach us the nuances of unconditional love.

Reincarnation is not an act of punishment – another concept not reflected in nature – but one human beings have embraced for millennia to imbue people with fear and respect for the authority administering the punishment. And what could be more convincing than assigning the punishment model to God? But unconditional love does not punish – it only seeks to teach.

On one level we may not really know what we are doing, or are doing something because we have been culturally conditioned to consider it acceptable: it may be expected of us to remain a loyal member of our clan. But the creator-in-training needs to experience the logical consequences of his creations if he is ever to learn and become the journeyman creator he is capable of becoming. He may need to learn that certain cultural norms are limiting and stifling his vision. They promote lazy love.

Think for a minute of a pastry chef. The creations that adorn a five-star resort Sunday Brunch did not emanate from the hands of a child picked randomly from the street. The skills of the Pastry Chef result from years of knowledge, both pastry- and non-pastry-related, and practice-failure-success cycles.

On a metaphysical level, our creative souls have to cycle through similar practice-failure-success trials to understand unconditional love. Otherwise, life is nothing more than an irrational lottery. Soul F gets born in Somalia in abject poverty. Soul P gets born an Inuit on the outskirts of the Arctic. Soul G gets born in San Francisco, California. What possible value could our individual and collective actions have if life is only a cosmic lottery? Why do we want peace? If we destroy the planet, who will notice? Who will care? Stars are exploding and disappearing all the time. What's one less celestial body?

The blood-line theory that takes us from Adam and Eve to 7 billion and counting human beings, argues the importance of our physical being. But that also would argue away any need for a soul. If it's all physical, a matter for mechanical, predictable birth-life-death processes, then what's this soul stuff? What would be the purpose of a soul? Survival of the fittest – the natural model – would further deny any functional need for a soul.

But if the soul is the permanent, forever aspect of our being, and physical existence a temporary assignment, then there's more to living than we humans have yet to imagine. I think it was Einstein who said, "God does not play dice with the universe." I believe him.

I have shared my story and insights hoping that they may provide a perspective that resonates with you. We are so conditioned from birth to conform to the mores and norms of the day; it sometimes takes a serious jolt to our story to look differently at things directly in front of us. And I have never seen a time in our human history that needs a different perspective on so many things we continue to recreate lifetime after lifetime that obstruct unconditional love and thwart world peace.

The answer to my prayer turned my world upside down, but I wouldn't go back – I couldn't go back – to the way I looked at life in 1991. I don't know how reincarnation works, but I don't fear death. I know that unconditional love is the only viable way to create our individual lives, our families, our communities, our business, and government entities. And I am still learning what unconditional love is: I still have much to grasp. Hopefully the karma of my abuses and choosing to ignore discrimination has been somewhat released, but that's something I won't know until I leave this planet.

I will try to live my remaining days in the most loving way possible, eschewing polarizing rhetoric of right and wrong, and being of service wherever I can. I will choose whenever I can, **not** to contribute any more fear-induced karma to my current liability and not participate in creating negative Karma with others. Instead, I will create Love.

Nor will I be silent. My intent is never to turn my back on abuse again and speak my truth whenever I have the opportunity, creating love and defusing fear.

Join me if you will. Be a ***Love Monger*** to model another perspective for the fear mongers who reside on every corner. Consciously choose to Create Love at every opportunity. We'll be that much closer to world peace if we do.

And wouldn't sooner be more loving than later?

The good news is there is no deadline.

# SOME SUGGESTIONS FOR CREATING LOVE AND BEING A LOVE MONGER

1.  Think about Love.

    Consider the common elements of love: parity, growth, beauty, joy, etc. How can love be applied to more than babies and romance? Politics? Religion? Euthanasia? Poverty? Cancer? Wealth? Abortion? Our Planet? Love and loving ways will be easier to recognize when we have consciously considered the nature of love and its myriad manifestations. It also will be easier to unmask fear.

2.  Teach love. Model love.

    We teach what we know. We cannot teach what we don't know. We can teach love and loving ways, only if we know love and loving ways. We will teach fear, violence, and abuse if that is what we know. Take stock in what you know and remain open and curious to other perspectives. Consider that the violent and the abusive may only know that response. Model another approach to help them learn.

3. Love yourself.

   Treat yourself in loving ways. You cannot genuinely love others if you don't love yourself. There is no limit to the number of people we can love: there is a finite amount of energy we can endure of those we fear and those who create fearful situations. Choose to surround yourself with those you deem loving and distance yourself from anyone who seeks to rob you of your loving energy, even if they are blood relatives.

4. Seek loving solutions.

   If you find yourself at a decision point, refrain from asking what the "right" thing is to do: ask instead what is the most "loving" response to the situation? Do not forget to include *yourself* in the equation that seeks a loving response.

5. Stay Curious.

   Never stop learning. We are capable of learning incredible amounts of information. We are capable of recognizing the destructive patterns in our lives and replacing them with more loving and supportive ones. Maintain an open mind. Be open to questioning everything: be prepared to unlearn those things that do not promote your well-being and the well-being of others.

6. Look past the role to the soul.

   Truly believe that we are equal souls on the stage of life; each having a part to play, but no one better or more deserving of love than any other, regardless of his station or status or geography in this lifetime. Just as stage plays and movies have leading and minor characters, with actors alternating between lead and minor roles: our souls alternate between major and minor roles through incarnations, and wear different costumes depending on the role. That all men are created equal speaks more to their eternal soul than the human character they have chosen to play in this lifetime. Look past the role to the soul.

7.  Refrain from judging yourself and others.

    Every time you judge, you continue to separate yourself rather than find kinship with the one you judge. Judging reinforces a not-so-subtle message that you are not good enough, or deserving enough for the love, joys and rewards of life, which is the fundamental message of your judgment.

8.  Refrain from negative communications.

    Just as telecommunication devices need repeaters to retain the viability of an analog message, in human communications, "repeaters" retain the positive or negative message we share within families, among nations, and in our thoughts. Choose to communicate loving messages: think loving thoughts as often as humanly possible. Choose to defuse the non-loving ones, by refraining from gossip, by refraining from ridicule and shamming, and by refusing to participate in organizations, institutions or families which perpetuate non-loving communications. Notice how often social media repeats negative and destructive messages. Refrain from participating or choose to *reframe* the discussion.

9.  Give children space to grow.

    Cultivate the soil around your children, but let them choose their own path. They instinctively know what it is they are prepared to do and be good at. Help them find it: don't dictate your biases about what's best for them.

10. Refrain from "pay back."

   Some abused human beings feel entitled to abuse their friends, spouse and children, in a perverted model of paying-it-forward. If you are a victim of abuse, acknowledge the abuse, even if you are unsure of the source, and seek help to interrupt and end the cycle.

11. Look for genius and inspiration everywhere.

   Creative consciousness is a human potential and our ability to find and recognize creative genius may reflect more poignantly on our personal receptors than in a lack of genius, inspiration or creativity in the world.

12. Seek non-polarizing communications.

   Notice how often the words "right" and "wrong" and their religious and political siblings are used by our culture. Try to find alternate words that communicate more effectively your loving intent and expectations. When we are polarized, we cannot find common ground. "War" – and each of its destructive expressions – is the natural outcome and will always be a barrier to peace.

13. Believe in Grace.

   I believe that grace includes the opportunity to learn through others' lessons. We do not have to murder someone to realize that violence is not a loving solution to a problem. We do not have to reincarnate into every conceivable combination of earthly bodies and personalities to recognize the most loving, life-sustaining alternatives. We can choose in this lifetime, to make life-altering changes based on intelligence and a conscious understanding of our interconnectedness to everyone and everything.

14. Believe that *All* human beings are created in the image of God.

    Your cosmic siblings include enemies, opposites, and kindred spirits. Every manner of human expression is a tryout and our collective reactions validate or reject the example. Validate love. Reject fear and abuse.

Margaret McElrath

# ABOUT THE AUTHOR

Margaret McElrath is retired from a 40-year career in Information Technology and lives in Williamsburg, Virginia, with her husband John. Their daughters also live on the east coast, while brothers, cousins and other relatives live on the west coast. Margaret graduated from Cal Poly, Pomona, with a BS degree in Language Arts. She has had a life-long interest in writing. As a young adult she was introduced to metaphysics by her father. A native Californian who grew up in a farming community, Margaret enjoys gardening, reading, and choral singing. Connect with her on Twitter @ LOVmonger and through her website: Cre8Lov.com.

www.ingramcontent.com/pod-product-compliance
Lightning Source LLC
Chambersburg PA
CBHW071610040426
42452CB00008B/1305